# Theories of Learning in Christian Education

# Theories of Learning in Christian Education

by

ROBERT R. BOEHLKE



THE WESTMINSTER PRESS
Philadelphia

LIBRARY OF CONGRESS CATALOG CARD NO. 62-14049

PRINTED IN THE UNITED STATES OF AMERICA

*To my wife, Mary*

*To my wife, Mary*

# Contents

# Introduction

WITH THE PIONEERING WORK of Edward L. Thorndike, the nature of learning became a distinctive subject of investigation in the field of psychology.[1] Thousands of experiments have been undertaken, and selective theories proposed, to reflect the evidence obtained.

The development of research and the proliferation of learning-theory reports have been observed with interest by Christian educators within the formal structure of the church. Literature released by denominational boards for teacher-training takes cognizance of so-called "laws of learning." At a pragmatic level these are helpful to teachers of the Christian faith within the church. However, functional effectiveness must also come to grips with theological validity. This element is absent whenever educators embrace selected theories of learning without going through the exacting discipline of examining the relationship between the theories of learning and the theology of the church. The importance of the problem of learning in Christian nurture is also neglected where Christians avoid confrontation with learning theory by developing theological approaches independently of it.

The meaning of learning theory for Christian nurture has not received the attention of many educators. Whether learning theory is deficient or adequate at this point is less an issue. What is important is that a serious attempt be made to understand learning theory from within the perspective of the church's faith and life. It is my judgment that no learning theory as now expressed has sufficient theological validity to be unconditionally accepted as the theoretical structure on which to build learning tasks for Christian nurture.

Therefore, the purpose of this book is to analyze learning theory, to evaluate it theologically, and to propose a theory of learning that reflects the most authoritative insights from learning theory and theology.

"Christian nurture" as a term is intended to describe the growth of the whole person through experiences of learning within the context of the church. The "church" includes the Christian family as well as the gathering of two or more such families organized as a corporate structure for nurture, worship, and mission. By Christian nurture, then, I mean the formal attempt of the church to provide learning opportunities for persons so that they can make intelligent responses to God's continuing act of grace.

Since the use of the term "learning" is at the center of this discussion, there must be clarity about its meaning. A definition of it must be sufficiently inclusive to provide for the expression of positions represented by various theories of learning and yet be exclusive enough to be useful for purposes of Christian nurture. In this study, learning is understood to be that dynamic process through which an individual is changed in relationship to a perceived situation. This view takes its reference from the vantage point of the person, but not a person as an individual in isolation. It is accepted that the most fundamental change may be in relationship to persons, events, situations, the world, and God. Changes may also occur in persons through maturation, by the effect of drugs, or by fatigue, but these changes do not involve learning and are, accordingly, not discussed.

Theory is understood as a statement or statements that attempt to summarize succinctly what has occurred and what ought to occur if similar conditions are present.

Therefore, learning theory is a statement or statements that seek to explain the process and the conditions through which learning may occur or be expected to occur.

Currently, learning theory divides into two principal families: the stimulus-response and the cognitive.

The stimulus-response family explains the process of change in the individual as the result of the establishment of bonds or connections between a stimulus and a response. When a response is elicited repeatedly in the presence of a given stimulus, learning is said to have occurred. If a substitute stimulus comes to elicit the same response as the original one, the process is known as " conditioning." However, the most influential variety of stimulus-response theory is not conditioning but " reinforcement " theory. Here the tendency to respond is held to be always dependent upon the response being rewarded.

Cognitive theory considers the stimulus-response explanation as oversimplified in depth and limited in scope. Instead, to learn, the learner must be able to see himself as involved within the problem to be solved or the understanding to be gained. Learning results from the restructuring of the learner's field of relationships by the learner himself and without the fumbling movements of trial and error associated with reinforcement theory. Learning also follows from the learner's ability to observe " what leads to what." These positions are represented respectively by gestalt and sign-gestalt theories.

When learning theorists attempt to meet the objections raised by other theorists, they are usually working at the basic question whether all learning may be subsumed under one explanation. Are different processes involved in the acquisition of skills and the gaining of knowledge? Here theorists are conversing with one another about the problem of " kinds of learning." The tendency has been for each theorist to assert that there is but one kind of learning, and this kind is described by his theory.

Certain attitudes and understandings are presumed to be

significant in the Christian faith. In distinction from kinds of learning, these issues are designated as "concerns to be learned." The concerns to be learned in Christian nurture must be answered by a kind or kinds of learning.

What the concerns to be learned are must await more intensive analysis and exposition. Only after the concerns are defined is it possible to evaluate whether learning theory is able to address itself to these concerns either functionally or theologically.

The four major learning theories — reinforcement, conditioning, gestalt, and sign-gestalt — will be probed to determine the key elements in each theory as well as its strengths and weaknesses. No attempt is made to deal with all the ramifications of learning theory because this has already been done in such thorough works as Ernest Hilgard's *Theories of Learning* [2] and W. K. Estes', *et al., Modern Learning Theory.*[3] Neither is there a discussion of personality and motivation theories except for evaluative purposes in terms of learning theory. Were these theories studied, the focus of the book would be altered beyond its intentions.

Once there has been an analysis of the adequacy of learning theory, however, the problem is only partially solved. The insights of theology must be brought to bear. Theology is that intellectual discipline which attempts to interpret the church's faith and life in relation to the Word of God as revealed in Jesus Christ, as witnessed to in the Scriptures, and as proclaimed by the church. Because the church's faith and life include the process of its nurture, theology has the obligation to present its original insights on process as well as to provide norms for evaluating learning theory. The task of theological validation is the examination of learning theory conclusions to see if they possess theological integrity for the concerns to be learned in Christian nurture.

Those divisions of theology assumed to have particular relevance for this study are the doctrines of revelation, man, the church, and the Holy Spirit. Other doctrines might be appropriate, but attention has been centered upon these four. (*a*) Process in Christianity cannot be discussed without being involved in God's action to make learning of the faith possible. Consequently, the meaning of God's self-disclosure in Jesus Christ must be investigated. (*b*) Since process has to do with persons as learners, man must be described from a theological perspective. His nature, his prospect for the experience of learning, and his destiny must be stated. (*c*) The church is a redemptive fellowship transforming selves in its care. Because this is true, process in Christian nurture must take cognizance of the church as the context of learning. (*d*) In the Christian faith, confession is made that the power to become Christ's faithful disciples rests in the power of God. Accordingly, a theory of learning must consider the place of the Holy Spirit in the process of Christian nurture.

After the doctrines have been studied in terms of Biblical and theological sources, implications for learning theory may be expressed. These understandings become the criteria for evaluating the theological validity of learning-theory solutions for the concerns to be learned in Christian nurture.

Since I do not consider current learning theory to be fully valid for Christian nurture, responsible criticism requires the hazarding of a new theory of learning. This is one which builds on the basic formulations of learning theory and theology. If the attempt is successful, it will be a theory of learning having theological integrity and psychological adequacy.

The movement of thought in this book, then, progresses in this way: Chapter I expresses representative solutions by Christian educators for the problem of learning in Christian nurture. Chapter II describes the concerns of Christian nurture which a theory of learning must explain. Chapter III presents and evaluates the major theories of learning. Chapter IV brings the theological resources into focus and draws implications from them for the process of learning. Chapter V is the central part of the book. The expository and analytic work has been finished. For the first time, Christian education, learning theory, and theology come into relationship. The result is a theological evaluation of learning theory for Christian nurture. Chapter VI sketches an outline of a theory of learning for the special nature of the Christian educational enterprise.

This book is based on the author's dissertation submitted to the faculty of the Princeton Theological Seminary in 1961 for the degree of doctor of theology. A microfilm of the dissertation is available through University Microfilms, Inc., 313 North First Street, Ann Arbor, Michigan. The manuscript has been revised at the invitation of The Westminster Press and because of the conviction that such a book will make a needed contribution to the literature on curriculum theory as this touches on the learning process.

While church school superintendents and teachers may find this book helpful, it is designed primarily for thinkers in Christian education theory at a professional level such as Christian education personnel in denominational boards, pastors, directors of Christian education, faculty and students of church colleges and theological seminaries, and scholars interested in conversation between learning theory and theology. It must be emphasized that this book is an investigation at the place of theory rather than practice. In other words, it is not intended to give immediate answers for problems that have just arisen within a church school class. Yet, if the rethinking in theory is pursued with diligence, improved practice should result. The dimensions of practice, however, cannot be dealt with in the limitations set by this study.

I am indebted to Dr. D. Campbell Wyckoff for first challenging me with the problem of learning theory as related to the unique needs of Christian nurture and for his guidance in the arduous task of writing the dissertation. Further words of appreciation must be expressed to the Graduate Study Fellowship Committee of The United Presbyterian Church in the United States of America for providing the grants that made the original study possible. Last, but certainly not least, I am grateful to my wife, Mary, for establishing the context of love and understanding in our home, and for carefully shepherding our three active children, Lisa, Eric, and Heidi, in order that the writing could proceed with a minimum of domestic distractions.

R.R.B.

*Stony Point, New York*

## Chapter I

# Learning Theory in Christian Education Thought

Carl Rogers has quoted Lewin to the effect that nothing is so practical as a good theory.[1] Lewin's comment is an apologetic against the inevitableness of conflict between theory and practice. He is asserting that without theory, practice lacks directions. Even the most "practical" person operates on the basis of theory whether this is articulated as such or not. Therefore, effort expended in thinking theoretically may be the most economical use of energy.

The process of theory-building is the attempt to penetrate to the heart of the matter. It is the result of dealing adequately with the ideas or phenomena to be explained in order to develop provisional guidelines for a particular situation. If the evidence on which the theory is built changes, the theory may be modified to include the additional data. In brief, the task of theory-building is the most responsible approach to the problems of practice. This is equally true for the field of Christian education.

Christian educational theory results from an orderly approach to the question of objectives, principles of curriculum, and principles of administration. Each of these components of educational theory grows out of a profound questioning of the foundational disciplines of philosophy, psychology, sociology, history, and, above all, of theology as the self-language of the living church informed and judged by the Word of God.

Christian education cannot use the raw findings from other fields. It asks educational questions of the other fields and receives answers in noneducational terms. Theory for Christian education builds on the evidences from various sources, but it exercises the right of prior jurisdiction for the reorganization of the material. Of course, no discipline does otherwise because it cannot depend upon itself for all information. Christian education borrows, but the borrowing is always restructured. In this sense, a new contribution is made. This means that educational theory in the church is other than a fixed body of facts once delivered. Since the theorist is one committed within the fellowship of the church, he struggles with the implications of the foundation disciplines for the needs of the present. The resulting theory is, accordingly, varied. However, the normative position of theology does not change. Educational theory reflects theology, and theology is captive to the Word of God. The ramifications of this rediscovery have been in the process of refinement in Christian educational thought, particularly since 1950.

But as was frequently the case in the rapid thrust of an armored column across enemy territory during World War II, pockets of resistance remained behind the most forward units. The major objective of a road junction or a bridge needed to be reached first. Later the pockets could be dealt with in order to preserve the victory. Christian education theory has left several areas of concern virtually untouched in its determination to develop objectives, curriculum principles, and principles of administration with due regard to the theology of the church.

One of the most significant areas of curriculum thought that has been bypassed is learning theory. People do learn various aspects of the Christian faith, but few educators have been troubled about the adequacy of general learning theory to meet the needs of Christian nurture. The Concordia Symposium observes that to the best of its knowledge no serious analysis has been made of learning theory in relationship to theology.[2] It appears that the time has now come for curriculum theory within Christian education theory to exercise vital concern about the foundations on which it is building opportunities for learning.

When faced with the problem of dealing with learning theory and theology, Christian educators have taken their stance chiefly on four main positions: (*a*) The process of learning in Christian nurture has been considered independently of learning theory. (*b*) Learning theory has been held to be compatible with theology and consequently valid for Christian nurture. (*c*) Learning theory has been held to be so lacking in refinement as to make a legitimate choice from among competing theories impossible. (*d*) Questions have been raised about the theological validity of learning theory for all of the concerns of Christian nurture.

To see how these positions have been worked out by contemporary Christian education theorists is our immediate objective. For the first time, a brief compendium on learning theory in Christian education will be readily available.

### Learning Separated from Learning Theory

To indicate that certain theorists have attempted to launch out in a fresh description of learning in Christian nurture without regard for the field of learning theory does not constitute a criticism per se. Christian education is indebted to these individuals for seeking new structures of thought. All approaches about to be surveyed grow out of a genuine grappling with theology as a source for answers to the problem of learning. However, as will become evident, the validity or the lack of validity of learning theory in Christian nurture has not been touched.

According to Reuel Howe, an abiding relationship is the most basic of human needs. This means that the problem of learning in the church's teaching ministry becomes an investigation of the process by which the message of God's love may be accepted by individuals. Stated in another manner, the problem in learning is to find an answer to the deep desire " to be at one with someone, to have someone who can be at one with us, and through whom we can find at-oneness with all." [3] This may be a psychological insight alone. Yet Howe prefers to say that if in fact God has created man to live in relationship, then this is no longer a psychological discovery. It is a theological one.[4]

The actual communication of God's acceptance of the unacceptable comes through the church's use of the language of relationship, the language of mutual address and response, the language of trust and love.[5] The individual's first experience of the church's language of relationship is the sacrament of Baptism. Here is God's testimony that he accepts the person even though the infant in this case cannot participate by verbal assent. The new relationship begun in baptism communicates the power of God in Christ for human salvation.[6] Beyond baptism, the language of relationship is still appropriate. Rote memorization may issue in the gaining of potentially enriching material such as the Apostles' Creed, the Lord's Prayer, and the Ten Commandments. But Howe contends that this is not Christian learning because the meanings taken to the self are always relative to the quality of relationships with persons. The egocentric man has used persons in other contexts of life. When he confesses " God " in the creed, he is likely to be thinking of God as a rather minor satellite rather than as the effective power of the universe. Another person has experienced trust and encouragement from others. He learns the meaning of the creed within the framework of a relationship of mutual confidence.[7] The importance of gaining information is not denied. Nevertheless, there is a greater risk that too much reliance is placed on the inherent possibilities of words alone where emphasis is on the acquisition of facts. Meanings do not reside in words themselves. Rather, they are related to the understanding of the person using the words.[8] Therefore, " Christian education must be personal; it must take place in a personal encounter and, only secondarily, is it transmissive." [9]

Charles Johnson presents a second theological approach to learning. This is learning which reflects Christianity defined as a relationship " between and among persons, both human and divine, at that deep level of interaction and interpenetration at which selves participate and communicate through the act of true self-giving (*agapē*) ." [10] The faith relationship described is experienced primarily and perhaps only within the redemptive community of the church.

The learning anticipated in Christian nurture is of such a character that it requires resources greater than those available within the human dimension. Learning is correlated with revelation, and revelation is God's disclosure of himself through Christ in the midst of man's anxieties about his human situation.[11] Because learning is dependent upon the divine initiative, it is subject neither to the manipulation of the educative process nor to the control of the educator. It is due to the grace of God. The integrity of human selfhood is preserved, however, because learning is a Subject-to-subject relationship. There is no sense of the false in the human response to revelation. Man is an active self responding to reality as he sees it. Johnson defends the involvement of the self in learning. " Because of the unique concern of Christian teaching with communication that can and does take place between selves, both human and divine, a dimension of relationship is involved in which the affirmation of the participating selves is a necessary concomitant to the changes [learnings] that occur." [12]

The learning resulting from true Christian nurture is more than the accretion of factual knowledge and more than spiritual growth. It is a radical transformation of the self.

Technically, Iris Cully does not use the term " learning

theory," but her exposition of the word " method " approximates what is discussed as learning theory. Certainly, she theorizes about the way the gospel is communicated. Only passing attention is given to a discussion of particular methods.

Learning in Christian nurture occurs through life-centered experiences understood as participation, recognition, and communication. " Life-centered " is defined as having a deep concern not only with the present but also with the past.[13] Learning through participation has more depth than learning by " doing." It means becoming involved in historic events and with persons as proclaimers of the gospel. " One can speculate *about* ideas; one tends to be drawn *into* events." [14] Learning through recognition suggests a mood of reverence as man encounters God. Man is addressed and makes response.[15] Encounter may occur through various learning tasks, but ultimately it is a divine decision. When the encounter has been followed by a response of faith, the outward sign is the commitment of the learner. Learning through communication is a matter of sharing ideas and deeds. It is an expression of basic learning. Learners are engaged in action because they are motivated to express their love for God who has redeemed them.[16]

## An Acceptance of Learning Theory

Jesse Ziegler's answer to the question of learning in Christian education is both original and traditional.[17] For this reason, he is related to both those who, dissatisfied with present learning theory, are breaking new ground and with those who consider the learning process to be quite well understood regardless of subject matter.

His originality is evident when he uses the word " encounter " to integrate a number of insights from the psychology of religion and from religious education.[18] Encounter means to meet. Persons learn in the encounter with the objective world, with culture understood as ideas and values, with persons, and with God. The most significant encounters postulated are ideas, values, and characteristics associated with, or embodied in, a person through the process of identification. This is not to say that the human characteristics will issue in encounter with God. No teacher can guarantee the divine-human encounter. He may only provide some of the conditions that may cause the encounter to be more likely.

For all of Ziegler's obvious strength in finding a way through the difficult terrain of learning theory, guidance is lacking for those who wish to move in the same general area. Learning of religion is held to be similar to other learning. There may be differences in content but " the essentials in education are the same." [19] This is a critical point which needs to be explored more fully.

Randolph Crump Miller finds reinforcement theory useful and appropriate for Christian nurture.[20] Learning demands the elements of drive, cue, response, and reinforcement.[21] Drive is related to motive, cue to stimulus, response to an act or thought and reinforcement to satisfaction obtained. The key to the whole process is reinforcement. Unless a response is rewarded immediately, there is no learning. After learning, there must be continued reinforcement, or earlier learning tends to disappear.

In Miller's brief treatment of learning, justification is offered for reinforcement theory on psychological rather than theological grounds. It is held that all learning occurs in the same way, and Christians ignore these facts of learning at their peril.[22] If there is no theological evaluation of reinforcement, neither is there any indication why reinforcement theory is chosen to the exclusion of other current explanations. In the absence of other theories of learning, Christian educators are invited to place their confidence in reinforcement theory as an unqualified description of learning.

It must be admitted that adoption of reinforcement

theory provides a simple resolution to the complex problem of learning in Christian nurture. However, the assumption of validity can be no substitute for a more intensive examination of the theological implications of reinforcement theory.

## A Discriminating Use of Learning Theory

D. Campbell Wyckoff does not think that the present stage of thought permits identification with any specific learning theory to the exclusion of others.[23] He prefers a discriminating use of learning theory. Particular theories answer to special needs, but no single theory is amenable to all the concerns to be learned.

Persons learn through four processes: perception, practice, problem-solving, and identification. Perception suggests the theoretical foundation of gestalt psychology with its emphasis on relating parts and wholes. Practice is related to connectionism and reinforcement theory. It has usually made use of the laws of readiness, exercise, and effect. Learning as a result of problem-solving is associated with the theory of John Dewey. Persons confronted with a baffling problem adopt and test hypotheses until a solution is achieved. This in turn may lead to other problems and the process continues. Depth psychology has contributed to an understanding of identification. As the learner identifies himself with admired persons, he takes the qualities of the latter to himself.[24]

The task of the Christian educator at this point in learning theory is to be clear about what is to be taught in terms of categories such as attitudes and skills. Each concern to be learned may then be related to specific theories of learning. A suggested breakdown is given.

"*Facts,* such as the events of the life of Jesus or the history of the church, might be learned either through perception or through practice, depending upon their context and use. Such methods as reading, study, discussion, analysis, memorization, and drill might be appropriate.

"*Ideas,* such as the Trinity or human destiny, might be learned best through perception, in which case methods like reading, study, and discussion could be used.

"*Skills,* such as prayer and worship, would require a good deal of practice, calling for analysis, memorization, and drill.

"*Other skills,* such as social action, would call for considerable problem-solving in addition to practice and would therefore involve the use of projects.

"*Habits* (closely related to skills), such as Bible study, might call for practice if they were narrowly conceived or might call for all types of learning if they were broadly conceived. This illustrates the difficulties involved in habit theories of learning.

"*Attitudes,* such as loyalty and love, might call for problem-solving and identification, thus using methods such as discussion, projects, meditation, other devotional acts, and music and the arts.

"*Appreciations,* such as understanding the Word of God and the meaning of the sacraments, would call for all four types of learning but would certainly not be complete without identification.

"*Values,* such as stewardship or discipleship, would seem to involve all four again but primarily perception, problem-solving, and identification. The chief Christian value, the life in Christ, is the most integral, demanding, and meaningful identification possible; it inextricably involves also identification with the church, his body." [25]

After examination of the means by which a learning theory may become the theoretical foundation for concerns to be learned, Wyckoff calls attention to the possibilities inherent in the learning task approach. According to the latter, learning is an experience of becoming that involves the five processes of "exploration (getting to know), discovery of meaning and value (understanding and appreciating), personal appropriation of meaning and value (making it one's own), conversion of meaning and value (confessing and accepting the gospel), and assumption of responsibility (doing things about it)." [26]

No learning theory is related to specific tasks, but it appears evident that the conception of learning grows out of learning-theory research. No assumption is made that learning theory is immediately appropriate. The form needs to be recast for the special issues of Christian nurture. Furthermore, the critical use of learning theory is qualified by the introduction of the words, "in the light of the gospel." This affirms that Christian educational theory must bring its own insights to the discussion of the problem of learning. Furthermore, the experiential emphasis indicates that the Christian view of man as self is preserved. Learning is not "something done to persons." It is the action of a responsible self experiencing his relationships.

The policy statement of the Curriculum Committee of The Methodist Church is also in substantial agreement with the discriminating use of learning theory. It is acknowledged that "there are a number of ways people learn, depending upon the nature of what is learned." [27] Persons learn by rote, conditioning, identification, trial and error or trial and success, and by insight.

Rote learning is useful for the acquisition of information, but it must be supplemented by attempts to understand what is memorized. Conditioning is a process often unconscious whereby children acquire the meanings and values of their culture. Yet, there are limits to conditioning because what is learned is dependent upon the nature of the teaching circumstances. Away from the environment of the Christian home, opposing values may also be learned. Through identification, persons take to themselves the qualities of a beloved person. If the loved person is Jesus Christ, identification becomes a most significant factor issuing in discipleship. But the admired person may also embody other than the life of quality. In this case, identification is a hindrance to the concerns of Christian nurture. Trial-and-error learning is described as similar to Dewey's problem-solving. It is especially appropriate in all forked-road situations where choices and decisions are imperative. Learning by insight is a matter of observing clues in a situation and relating them in a new way.[28]

The discriminating use of learning theory by Wyckoff and the policy statement of The Methodist Church are two expressions of thought that are moving in the right direction. Although theological compatibility is not investigated, there are numerous hints that theological insights modify the usefulness of a particular learning theory. This arrangement is functionally valid, but the deeper problem of theological validity in learning theory remains to be determined. Such an analysis is the purpose of this book.

### A Critical Evaluation of Learning Theory

According to Howard Grimes, Christian education learning theory must be conceived as pluralistic rather than monistic. He writes that "learning is a process involving the total spectrum of influences that make a person what he is. Learning . . . in the church is a much broader enterprise than we have sometimes believed."[29] It involves trial and error, conditioning, rote, and insight. Instead of accepting all theories as equally authentic for Christian nurture, Grimes weighs the theological implications of the particular theory.

The validity of trial-and-error learning is accepted but without suggesting concerns in Christian nurture where it is especially appropriate. Reservations are expressed about conditioning because the theological understanding of man does not permit control of one person by another.[30] This does not mean that conditioning is itself invalid as a theory of learning. The church recognizes that conditioning is continuing at all times, but the church ought not base its nurture on it. Rote learning is partially valid as a theory of process. Christian teaching must impart a knowledge of the Bible and of the Christian heritage. Yet the church must not depend upon rote learning because nurture demands an understanding of the faith. Insight learning has theological integrity. Modified as personal and creative encounter, it becomes the most adequate theory of learning in the church. Through it, there is a possibility of accounting for the more basic learning anticipated in Christian nurture. Grimes expresses it this way: " From a Christian point of view, nothing has really been learned until it affects one personally [' existentially '] in terms of his relationships with the God and Father of our Lord Jesus Christ." [31]

Lewis J. Sherrill's discussion of the relationship between learning theory and theology has been the most extensive treatment to date.[32] He has raised serious questions about the theological integrity of learning theory for Christian nurture. Although just brief expositions and evaluations are offered of conditioning, trial and error, and insight learning, these are important for Christian education theory.

Conditioning is useful for indicating some of the clues of human interaction. " This principle leads us to be aware that the response which a pupil makes is the response which he is learning; this actual response may be what we desire, or it may be very far from it; but in either case he is learning what he is doing." [33] There must be theological reservations about conditioning because of its tendency to elevate the mechanics of learning at the expense of the selfhood of the person. The teacher working under the structure of conditioning " easily degenerates into a manipulator of the pupil, treating him as a thing to be experimented with and shaped according to some blueprint." [34]

Trial-and-error learning is based on the fact that in a new situation, learners make a series of random movements until the right one is achieved. If reward follows, the response is likely to be repeated. Trial-and-error learning has validity for Christian education especially where habits are under consideration. However, habits must be kept under scrutiny because they may prevent confrontation with God.[35] Again, trial-and-error learning may violate the theological understanding of selfhood. The learner is approached from the outside as if he had no interior life of his own to command. Motivation for change is considered the responsibility of the teacher. Dewey's problem-solving is a type of mental trial-and-error learning and is valid for Christian education in two respects: It stresses the person's own experiences in the process of learning and it holds that learning occurs within a social milieu. " Both of these values . . . are very close to the human side of the New Testament conception of knowing by experience within the koinonia." [36] Dewey's problem-solving is also invalid for Christian education because it is unable to deal with the demonic element in the human creature and in society, and because of its emphasis upon the pragmatic nature of truth. This may lead people to find " that the conception of truth in the form of a Person who is seeking *them* has been obscured or even completely lost." [37]

Learning by insight is theologically compatible. It is a corrective to trial-and-error learning by showing that the learner is able to find a solution to the problem situation by prompt adaptation of means to ends. Insight learning is especially adequate to explain situations where moral and spiritual confusion prevail. In those moments, purpose is discovered and a shift in the self may occur which is " so radical as to give one the feeling and the conviction that a new self is coming into being." [38]

What, then, is the status of learning theory in Christian education literature? Some educators have proceeded to an exposition of a learning theory for Christian nurture without regard to the existence of the field of learning theory. This has resulted in a body of literature to be evaluated for its functional as well as theological adequacy, but it has not met the need for a basic theological and psychological understanding of learning as it is found in the church.

Among other educational theorists, learning theory has been accepted as an accomplished fact. In some cases, a particular learning theory is appropriated without asking about its theological implications or its functional usefulness. This type of exposition is not keeping pace with the development in other phases of curriculum theory.

In reaction to the fluid state of learning theory but with appreciation for the field itself, theorists have tried to be discriminating in their use of learning theory. The concerns to be learned are analyzed to determine which theory will be most complete. In the main, the discussion of theological criteria is not brought to bear in this investigation.

Finally, some thinkers have faced the issue of theological validity in learning theory for Christian nurture. Literature on this subject is still in swaddling clothes, as it were. More students need to become interested in order that through analysis, evaluation, and discussion, a reservoir of thought for learning theory in Christian nurture may result. The remaining chapters are intended as a contribution to this end.

## CHAPTER II

# Concerns to Be Learned

THE PROBLEM of learning theory is complicated by the near-hallowed view that all learning occurs in the same way. This has been the unchallenged axiom by which learning theorists have attempted to account for the varied changes in human behavior as the result of learning. The " law " of parsimony has been as rigid as " the laws of the Medes and Persians which altereth not "!

Now there are signs that this position is being questioned. It is suggested that there is no such thing as learning theory in general. There can only be a theory of learning that accounts for the relationships of a particular situation. Norman R. F. Maier writes that " the fact that an animal shows insight in a maze does not mean it must behave insightfully in a puzzle box. May not random behavior and insightful behavior be different in kind? " [1]

Arthur Melton's procedural recommendation is illustrative of the changing view for the determination of the range of applicability of an individual theory. " We cannot hope to have a general theory of human learning until we can describe systematically the similarities and differences of the tasks and behaviors involved in the wide variety of learned behavior exhibited by human subjects, because until we can do that it is impossible to relate the effects of procedural variables, such as motivations, incentives, reinforcements, distributions of practice . . . to the characteristics of the task or situation." [2]

Ernest Hilgard, too, wonders whether there are common laws to account for such diverse processes as the acquisition of motor skills, memorization of a poem, solving a geometrical puzzle, and understanding a period of history.[3] In calling for a more satisfactory theory, he writes, " we need a more careful delineation of the *kinds* of learning which take place [each of which may have ' laws ' of its own], and an acceptable fractionation of the *aspects* of learning which make demands upon theory." [4] In terms of Christian nurture, attention must be given to the determination of those concerns which are to be encompassed by a theory of learning. Until the concerns to be learned are known, there is no way to know whether a particular theory of learning is either functionally or theologically adequate.

Were the broad categories of concerns to be learned at the immediate disposal of Christian education theory, this chapter could be omitted. But such is not the case. Literature in Christian education theory discusses objectives and curriculum principles, but the frame of reference does not require the listing of concerns to be learned. Now such a classification is imperative. On the basis of a rather careful analysis of Scripture from the standpoint of nurture and recent basic works in Christian education theory, as well as personal conviction, seven concerns to be learned emerge to be answered by learning theory. These clusters of learning are: knowledge, understandings, attitudes, values, skill-habits, motives, and changes in the self.

There follows now an amplification of what is suggested by each classification. The description of each concern is not intended to be *exhaustive*. It is to indicate *direction* of meaning.

## Knowledge

As a term for grouping a type of concern for Christian nurture, " knowledge " is not used in the technical sense as a category of traditional philosophy. No questions are raised about the nature of ultimate reality, or about the infallibility of knowledge, or even about the means of grasping ultimate reality. An epistemological approach to the problem of process in Christian nurture is a distinct possibility and has been suggested by Albert Bailey.[5] However, knowledge is not being treated here in the manner envisaged by him.

Knowledge is an umbrella word covering informational subject matter. It may have been possible to use " facts " in this respect, but the term is not sufficiently inclusive. Other data should be learned that cannot be so narrowly defined. Concepts, such as redemption or justification, should be learned. These are part of the vocabulary of the Christian life. Yet it is not quite accurate to speak of concepts as facts even though they may be factual. Therefore, knowledge summarizes the basic data to be mastered. These have no primacy in themselves or the Christian faith would be reduced to a gnosticism. Knowledge describes some of the necessary tools for discipleship since the Christian faith involves a message to be communicated.

The foundation of Christian nurture is rooted in the divine election. This is not the wishful dreaming of a distant deity. It is the involvement of God with man in a series of mighty acts. This is clearly summarized in Ps. 105. In a spirit of worship as the response to what God has done on behalf of Israel, the psalmist sings: " Seek the Lord and his strength, seek his presence continually! Remember the wonderful works that he has done, his miracles, and the judgments he uttered " (Ps. 105:4-5). There follows a recital of God's relationship with Israel beginning with Abraham and continuing through the gift of the Land of Canaan. The mighty acts of God are understood by the Christian educators studied as particularly related to the movement of God to man as witnessed to in the Old Testament. Christians in the present generation need to claim their full heritage of faith. Ancient Israel's history is the modern Christian's history. There, man's sin is revealed.

There, God is known as a participating director of the drama of redemption. Only the first act is played, but intimations are present for what is to come. Throughout the Old Testament there is the overwhelming testimony that God acts in concrete events of personal, national, and international history.

Even as God's mighty acts are a descriptive summary of the essential content of the Old Testament, so God's act in Jesus Christ is specifically associated with the New Testament. The Christian faith rests on more than a factual base, but it cannot be less. At a particular point in world history, that is, during the reign of Caesar Augustus, God was incarnate in a son born of Mary. This one called Jesus passed through the challenges of childhood and youth. He attained manhood in the Galilean village of Nazareth. At about the age of thirty, he began to teach, preach, and live the Kingdom of God. He gathered a small company of persons about him. Later he was rejected by the religious leaders of Judea and was put to death as a criminal outside Jerusalem during the procuratorship of Pontius Pilate. But death could not hold him. On the first day of the week, he rose from the dead and was seen by many. He remained with his disciples for forty days before ascending to the Father. Such is the data of the Christian faith. Nurture fails to be thorough if the historical aspects of the life of Christ are disregarded. Mrs. Cully expresses a concern about the legitimate place of information in the Gospel narratives as the kerygma. " It is historically oriented. It depends for its cogency and its appeal on the fact that it rests on certain well-attested historical data. It is not myth; it is not a set of ideas. The Gospels were written to bear witness to God's revelation in Jesus Christ and to bring their hearers into faith. This kerygma is the foundation of the teaching within the fellowship of the church." [6]

Christian nurture intends to avoid the position of those early disciples whom Paul met at Ephesus. When asked if they had received the Holy Spirit when they believed, they replied, "No, we have never even heard that there is a Holy Spirit" (Acts 19:2b). None of the educators is satisfied that a knowledge about the Holy Spirit is sufficient. But all agree that Christian nurture to be Christian must be informed by the Holy Spirit. By implication, there is need to know about the Holy Spirit even as it is more essential to know him. Howe affirms the necessity of the Holy Spirit without equivocation. "Christianity is Trinitarian."[7]

Knowledge about God in his mighty acts, his revelation in Jesus Christ, and the fact of the Holy Spirit reaches a focal point in the faith and life of the church. The history of the church is the autobiography of a living organism. Appreciation of the present life of the church is dependent upon a knowledge of its glory, shame, defeats, and victories. Unless there is instruction about the church's history, the present generation may consider the church to be dependent upon each momentary confession of faith rather than as a continuing life. History is but one fact of the church, however. There must be a knowledge of the church's nature, its faith as evidenced in theology, its order as expressed through churches, its worship, and its mission.

To be sure, the church is persons. But the individual may be lost in the mass. Therefore, Christian nurture is concerned about a frank study of the nature of man. This involves man as created in the image of God and man as sinner. In addition to a theological knowledge of man, it is also imperative to see him in his psychological and sociological dimensions. At a more personal level, knowledge of man becomes knowledge of the self. Knowing one's identity does not assure change in outlook, but it is a precursor to a responsible view of oneself.

Christian nurture seeks no narcissistic complex. Self-reflection may issue in paralysis. Discipleship requires information about the social structure in which persons live. Vieth's study on objectives in religious education makes this clear as he lists one objective as " to develop in growing persons the ability and disposition to participate in, and contribute constructively to, the building of a social order embodying the ideal of the Fatherhood of God and the brotherhood of man." [8] This means learning to interpret the social order from a Christian perspective and to participate in social action. Prior to the realization of either of these goals is an awareness of the sociopolitico-economic order as now constituted and as it might become in the light of the gospel.

Appreciation of the social world in which we live is dependent upon a knowledge of non-Christian societies and religions. Instead of judging all other cultures as inferior because they are different, there may be the basis for making sympathetic but critical evaluations as a prelude to sharing the Christian gospel. Eugene Nida's works certainly undergird Christian educators' insistence on knowledge before action. His *Message and Mission* abounds with illustrations of the need for a knowledge of the social and religious structure of the community if communication is to be effective.[9]

The meaning of knowledge for Christian nurture is effectively pointed up in Sherrill's criticism of those who are fearful of all indoctrination. " They have felt it necessary to indulge in all sorts of methodological devices so as to skirt around frankly giving instruction." [10] Without basic expressions of knowledge, Christian nurture neither knows its religious heritage nor the setting in which discipleship is to be lived.

### Understandings

Immediately after expressing the necessity of knowledge as a concern to be learned, its insufficiency must be acknowledged. Learning as transmission of facts, information, and ideas does not deal with matters of interpretation. Verbalizing about knowledge may issue in the illusion that the learner is aware of what is meant by the ideas used.

The learner is in need of guidance to perceive what the facts, information, and ideas may mean in relationship with himself, with other selves, the world, the church, and God. Without understanding, it would be impossible to meet the unfamiliar situations which arise or to see wider implications of Christian teaching other than in the immediate context. The prophet Isaiah voiced the despair of God: " my people does not understand " (Isa. 1:3b) . " Understanding," then, indicates a learning to transform individual facts into constellations of experience. These are more than the sum of the factual material. They are a new whole that could not come into being apart from the facts but which go beyond the facts themselves.

One of the tasks of Christian education is to offer entrance into the inner structure of Biblical faith and life because Christian nurture is Biblically oriented. This is more than the development of encyclopedic proficiency. After data have been marshaled, questions of meaning persist. The writer of Deuteronomy speaks of a mature learning in the home. When the son comes and inquires about the meaning of the details associated with prevailing religious practices, the answer is given, " We were Pharaoh's slaves in Egypt; and the Lord brought us out of Egypt with a mighty hand " (Deut. 6.21) . God's redemption becomes the theme to draw together the separate strands of Israel's history. Instead of resting with confidence in the child's awareness of facts, the head of the family takes such action as permits an understanding of the details. The significance of understanding as a concern to be learned continues in modern Christian educational thought. Miller describes the Biblical drama of redemption as consisting of five acts: creation, covenant, Christ, church, and consummation.[11] These may be memorized, of course, but this does not issue in understanding. The five themes present a convenient device for probing and relating Biblical events at a deeper level of personal involvement. Persons should come to learn the meaning of God's history with man. This is as different from knowledge learning as is perceiving the meaning of life from an analysis of man's biological processes.

Revelation is a further aspect of understanding as a concern to be learned. Sherrill draws a careful distinction among the various forms in which revelation touches the human learner. The person may be content to describe the "fact" of revelation — God has disclosed himself. When the attempt is made to relate what the disclosure has meant, revelation has become a "report" and at least once removed from the original confrontation. Later, as individuals seek to correlate facts and reports, the "doctrine" of revelation may result.[12] At each position beyond the factual stage, the learner is invited to perceive the meaning of revelation for himself. Unless he learns to perceive what is disclosed, the disclosure has not touched him. "For to perceive is more than merely 'seeing' what is manifested, and it is more than 'hearing' what is uttered. One can see and not perceive; one can hear, and not understand." [13]

The facts on which the church's nature, history, worship, and mission are based do not change. However, the reaction of the community of believers to the facts varies from generation to generation. This implies that the church's nurture cannot be content with a transmissive function. It must provide opportunities for a learning to perceive meaning as responsible members of the church at a particular hour. Perfectly good terms such as the "new Israel," or the "body of Christ," or the "community of the Holy Spirit," need reinterpretation or there is likely to be spiritual stagnation. This accounts for the studies on the church in ecumenical councils. Nevertheless, if each communion repeats its own historic interpretation of the church as truth once delivered, there is no growth in understanding. There is only rote parroting of phrases. This is a level of activity which does justice neither to the mental faculties of man nor to the self-disclosure of God. A tape recorder would be as effective! Only as persons learn to risk their own prejudices and to enter freely into a study of the church is there a learning to understand. This is a vocation of Christian nurture. It reflects the highest concern for man. Persons are engaging in discovery of meaning at the point where they can give themselves to the church without sacrificing their intellectual integrity.

Christian educators also envision persons coming to understand themselves. This again is more than an analysis of data. Knowledge of the self and conditions which affect the self are like so many pieces of a puzzle. The pieces may be counted and even classified but until they have been rearranged, there is no cogent pattern. The numerous events of our lives, the personalities evidenced, and the state of estrangement from God and our fellows must be brought into relationship. As we learn more of the processes by which relationships are affected, we are on the threshhold of having our behavior radically altered.

Understanding as a concern to be learned in Christian nurture enters in at the place where vexing and challenging problems of human life arise. Clear-cut answers are not available even though there are foundations on which decisions may be based. What should be a person's life philosophy? How shall he react to the various periods of his life, such as childhood, youth, choosing a vocation, marriage, parenthood, retirement, and old age? If this is God's world, how do we account for the existence of evil and the resulting human suffering? Every person must experience death. It is not a foregone conclusion, however, that death will be perceived as the gateway to life unless there has been growth in learning to understand the problems which death brings to persons and the strategic Christian witness at this point.

A further cluster of situations that calls for a learning to understand is that of relating the relevance of the gospel for all the social structures. This means perceiving the relationship between the depth of commitment and the intricacies of social living. Here is a difficult task. It is hard to be objective about social issues unless these do not involve us existentially. If we are under threat by a social group because of real or imagined causes, something more than an awareness of issues is required. We are under constraint to learn how to bring the judgment and grace of the gospel to bear where we are. Howe draws the issue with precision. " Unless the vitality born of the meeting between God and men in worship finds expression in the issues of living, then personal relations, individual or social, are doomed. And the church . . . will be responsible." [14]

## Attitudes

Knowledge of God's revelation in Jesus Christ is presupposed for all Christian nurture. Yet knowledge may be acquired without changing the person's outlook. In a similar fashion, there may be deep understanding of the meaning and potential of the gospel but without personal involvement. Antagonists may understand perfectly the issues which divide them but without any disposition for a modification of their behavior. Therefore, attitude learning becomes another basic concern to be learned in Christian nurture.

Attitude learning engages the person's action processes to the extent that outward behavior conforms to norms of a group, tradition, or personal conviction. Christian nurture anticipates the development of attitudes that proceed beyond the identifiable action or the predisposition for action. This qualification anticipates a separation to be made more specific shortly between an attitude as a fit mark of a gentleman and one which is appropriate for Christian nurture. Miller puts it aptly. " Many church schools have turned out those who think they can be saved by keeping the law or by getting along with others, but actually all we have turned out have been Pharisees or Sadducees." [15]

Two principles are essential if attitude learning in Christian nurture is to be worthy of its name. Any attitude considered desirable must be seen in relationship to the divine grace. Church school curriculum units that stress a surface moralism of "sharing" and "being helpful" are deficient. Bible stories such as the little boy sharing his food with Jesus provide examples for conduct. These stories as often used suggest that the attitude under discussion is fully within the province of the child's will without regard for God's initiative in Jesus Christ.[16] Secondly, attitude learning in Christian nurture must recognize the demonic element in the teacher-learner-social relationship. Stating goals of attitude and conduct without regard for the fact of sin is evidence of gross naïveté.

With the two principles of God's grace and the demonic element in man kept to the fore of our thinking, it is feasible to speak of responsible nurture issuing in God-related attitudes.

The one consummate attitude that must be evident if Christian nurture is to reflect its origin in God is self-giving love, *agapē*. It is the central conviction that guides the Christian life. An *agapē* attitude is selfless devotion for another's well-being for the sake of Christ. "In this is love, not that we loved God but that he loved us and sent his Son to be the expiation for our sins. Beloved, if God so loved us, we also ought to love one another." (I John 4:10-11.) *Agapē* begins in God and returns to God through persons. A missionary to Uganda learned this meaning of love in her trials with a fellow worker. "To love a human being means to accept him, to love him as he is. If you wait to love him till he has got rid of his faults, till he is different, you are only loving an idea. He is as he is now, and he is to be loved now, as he is." [17] This is the goal. We want to love but find that we are handicapped. The one who needs our love is usually at that moment most unlovable. Instead of receiving love, he experiences rejection. "Our unlovableness becomes for him our unlovingness so that he not only does not get the love that he needs, but he gets an unlovingness that he does not need." [18] The realization of *agapē* fails at the human record of achievement. If real love is to be a possibility in personal relationships, it will be through God in Christ. Therefore, *agapē* as an attitude is a concern to be learned, but it is one which is approached with an awareness both of human limitations and divine sufficiency.

To have begun a discussion of some of the attitudes to be learned with the consummate *agapē* does not imply that it occupies an initial position in a hierarchy of learning. No more is intended than to express the primacy of love as an attitude according to Christian education theorists.

Another cluster of attitudes is associated with the word " penitent." Whether the learning process is experienced suddenly or over a period of time, the penitent attitude is the cornerstone on which future learnings may be structured. The proud man struggles to maintain his fortress-self against all encroachments without making judgments between friend and enemy. Until the learner's defenses are lowered, God remains an antagonist. But once God gains admittance to the self, the penitent attitude is in process of being learned. " The sacrifice acceptable to God is a broken spirit; a broken and contrite heart, O God, thou wilt not despise." (Ps. 51:17.) This is not like a fact which may be learned once for all. Humility characteristic of penitence must be learned again and again. The penitent person learns to repent of his sin. While he never fully succeeds in acknowledging his sin without sensing confession as a threat to himself, he nevertheless learns to confess. God comes to him not as an abstract power of love and goodness but as a person to whom the learner may turn deliberately. The attitude of penitence is set apart from easygoing conceptions of nurture as a continuing achievement of morality without the traumatic effect of repentance and the cathartic acceptance of Christ. The penitent attitude is basic nurture and basic to nurture. It has the wider implications of a willingness to be taught by God and to wait with expectancy for him. Far from being downcast, the penitent man has the confident joy of knowing that he does not need to carry the world's burden alone. "In returning and rest you shall be saved; in quietness and in trust shall be your strength." (Isa. 30:15.) Here is the prophetic expectancy that God is ever about to reveal himself in circumstances of the present.

If penitence is the attitude which frees the self to live in confidence with God, gratitude is the extension of the self in concrete acts and responses to God's gift of himself as Father, Son, and Holy Spirit. Persons are not grateful because this is the way they should be. One gift may lead to the desire for another. Parents in our affluent society know this well. Merchandising geared to the children's market expects that its appeal will find ready responses. If the item is purchased, does this mean that the child is automatically happier? Hardly. Available products become the child's due rather than the parent's gift. Gratitude must be learned even in the ordinary ventures of family life. It is not otherwise with God's dealing with us. Christian nurture anticipates that persons should learn the meaning of gratitude not analytically but existentially. God has so lavished himself upon us that the appropriate response is the breaking of many a jar of precious ointment in his behalf. (Cf. Mark 14:3-9.)

The Christian educational writings investigated are at one with regard to the development of attitudes issuing in grateful worship. Man may worship out of fear of the numinous. This is not gratitude. True worship in praise of God, in listening to his word, and in prayer arises in relationship to the greatness of personal redemption. The stewardship of life is also related to gratitude. Carefully conducted campaigns can extort funds from unwilling saints, but where gratitude is learned, persons give gladly of themselves and of their means because of their love for God. Christian nurture seeks to rescue gratitude from the market place and return it to the altar. Gratitude is a necessary concern of Christian nurture not because it pays but because it is right in the sight of God.

Another area to be explored may be identified as a responsible attitude toward life. It includes aspects that are not easily expressed but are related to the supremacy of the spiritual over the physical. The author of Deuteronomy first stated it in its Biblical context and Jesus reaffirmed it in the temptation account. "And he humbled you and let you hunger and fed you with manna, which you did not know, nor did your fathers know; that he might make you know that man does not live by bread alone, but that man lives by every thing that proceeds out of the mouth of the Lord." (Deut. 8:3.) Vieth calls attention to it as an objective of religious education: "To lead growing persons to build a life philosophy on the basis of a Christian interpretation of life and the universe."[19] Christian nurture considers it essential for persons to evidence growth in "a genuinely Christian spirit and attitude toward personal goals and human relationships."[20] But the achievement of a responsible attitude toward life is confused by a basic problem in identification. God created persons to be loved and things to be used. Apart from a change in attitude, we are prone to reverse this order by loving things and using persons.[21]

Attitude learning must not be approached as so-called "character education" unless the theological perspective infuses the entire venture. Ernest Ligon admits that his work is not concerned with theology, but he thinks it is possible to have character education without theology.[22] This view is not shared by the educators studied. Attitudes of the Christian life must be learned in relationship to the full implications of the gospel or they are sub-Christian.

## Values

Value as a concern to be learned represents an attempt by Christian educators to acknowledge that there is a realm of worth that should be taught. How shall worth be defined? Do the basic concerns of persons occur on the same level? To whom or to what shall persons give themselves?

Philosophically, idealism's value answer is most congenial with the meaning of value in Christian education theory. This is not to commit every Christian educator to the whole idealist position. But it is a matter of making fundamental decisions about the nature of value. For idealism, value is that which has existence and is perceived by sentient beings. J. Donald Butler has defined the idealist position in these words: "We enjoy values, not only because our emotions and sentiments are appropriately aroused so that we have certain desirable feelings, but *because the things we value are realities which have existence* themselves and are rooted in the very structure of the cosmos." [23]

None of the educators is willing to say with realism that whatever is the object of human desire has value.[24] This would remove Christian education from the scene where responsible judgments are made. It would prevent the expression of a view of value in relationship with the gospel message to be taught. If value is only that which is of present interest to a person, then there is no qualitative difference between the attention a hungry animal gives to a receptacle of possible food and the commitment of a person to God through the church. Value-as-food disappears until hunger pains are again felt. Value is then ephemeral. It has no necessary existence beyond the experience of the present.

Neither are Christian educators ready to describe value in the fashion of pragmatism as moving in the free flux and change of all experience. What a person thinks of a particular goal object is of less significance than the meaning of value for society. In pragmatism, "value is better described as being satisfactory to the situation than as being satisfying to the person or persons involved in the situation." [25] But value is less transient than in realism. Value is related to the future as well as the present.

With philosophic value in the background, it can be seen that Christian education is committed to the communication of concerns which are ultimate rather than relative. The values that should be learned are those which make a transcendent difference in a person. Perceived in this way, value learning provides resources for making critical judgments about personal, interpersonal, and social relationships. In the final analysis, the way the problem of value is answered and consequently learned touches on issues of life and death, life or death for the learner. This is true because God has revealed himself as one who is value. Only in relationship with him may enduring value be realized.

If it is true that God is value, then his ministering community in the world, the church, must also partake of his worth. Such, of course, is the Christian claim. The church may be localized for worship in a particular building. It may be deeply enmeshed in the culture of the day. Nevertheless, the church transcends its earthly limitations because the entirety of its life is permeated by the Spirit of God. The church is the divine community on earth. To come to feel strongly about the worth of the church is a basic concern of Christian nurture. But the value concern must be identified in terms of the church's nature. Otherwise, the exigencies of the moment may cause educators to lower their sights. In order to maintain an institution, value education may focus on the worth of manifestations of the church's life. There is value in a particular religious tradition. There is value in the church's program for children, youth, and adults. There is value in the quality of the professional staff. For many adults, the church as value never moves beyond this expression. Consequently, when the staff disappoints expectations, or when the program is deficient, no problem of conscience is encountered in a search for a church that more nearly meets values by the individuals. Now the church is captive to the horizontal dimension. Value is related to answering personal needs without regard to the church's divine origin. But the church must be learned as value because it is through this community of God that the gospel of reconciliation is ever communicated. Apart from the gospel, the church has no reason for existence. In this community, God is revealing himself. Precisely because here God is fashioning a people after his desire, the church must be learned as value. From this perspective, the church's worth is rooted more in the God who persists than in the changing needs and desires of persons.

As the church is learned as value, persons are encouraged to feel deeply about the life in Christ as the basis for personal action. This is no searching after ethical standards congenial with self-expression. No one needs the Christian faith to live a passably ethical life. Confusion at this point has led many to equate an acceptable code with the Christian faith. This does not begin to appreciate the value of the life in Christ. To be in Christ is to so value him that he is the beginning, continuation, and end in a hierarchy of values. Persons need to develop a point of view and a set of values that originate from God's act in Jesus Christ. Instead of having a delineation of values of varying permanence, there may be the perspective from which enduring value may be determined. Near the end of his life, Paul could say, " Indeed I count everything as loss because of the surpassing worth of knowing Christ Jesus my Lord" (Phil. 3:8a). He had found value related to God himself. Having learned something of the worth of the life in Christ, it is only another step to see implications of this value orientation for personal and social relations. Persons are more important than things because persons are created for fellowship with God. They have value in virtue of God's election.

We value persons not for what they can do to serve us but for what they are in themselves. If persons have value in Christ, this means also that social justice has intrinsic validity. It is not a concession which the majority grants to the minority. It is the minority's due because in Christ ordinary distinctions pass away. Non-Christian social movements may alleviate wrongs, and we may be grateful for them, but these lack authenticity if value is not seen as growing out of the very nature of God. It is this kind of value learning which becomes another manifestation of concerns to be learned in Christian nurture.

In terms of personal appropriation, value learning is accompanied by strong emotional overtones. This must be so because man is more than intellect and muscle. He is also feeling. He may feel strongly about the church and the primacy of the life in Christ. But he may also learn another aspect of both through art forms. To the extent that these express themes grounded in the nature of God, they may participate in and communicate value. Mrs. Cully upholds this position when she writes: "Art tries to go beyond the outward appearance in order to convey inner meaning. This can be a rich medium for revealing the depths of the Christian faith and of expressing the kerygma with power." [26] This is also the strength of symbolism in all art.[27] If the art form is a sign, that is, something arbitrarily chosen, it does not have value as the term is used here. However, if the form is a symbol, and therefore intrinsically related or participates in the reality to which it points, then the expressed art may be perceived as value. Through great art, the veil around reality has been drawn aside and we are able to "see." Christian nurture is concerned about helping persons learn to appreciate the unseen through the seen. Appreciation is understood as becoming existentially involved rather than as standing back and "liking" or "disliking" the painting, sculptured piece, music, literature, or dramatic form. Because art may be value, the person is confronted with a situation that demands a decision of eternal significance. Anyone who enters into Grünewald's grotesque painting, *The Crucifixion* of the Isenheim Altarpiece, or into the disintegrating world of Picasso's *Guernica,* or into the naked revelation of self in Camus's novel *The Fall,* cannot be indifferent.

Before these, man participates in value because they call him to recognize his desperate need for God.

### Skill-Habits

Technically, an argument could be made for a distinction between skills and habits, but none is being made. Rather, they are considered as different aspects of one concern to be learned.

Skills represent economy of action patterns. Inefficient physical movements or thought sequences are eliminated until a smooth operation remains. When the acquired skill is likely to recur with consistency in response to a situation or to personal will, the skill has become a habit. It is such a part of the person himself that he is virtually unaware of the complicated sequences which have resulted in the action. The situation calls for certain action or thought patterns and these are expressed without the formerly laborious and even traumatic experience of the initial learning. The action patterns are now either automatic or nearly so.

Skill-habits, motor and mental, are essential for the expression of the Christian faith. Lack of skill in presentation of the gospel may prevent persons from hearing God's voice. The gospel in this case is rejected because the vehicle is unacceptable. Persons must learn to worship, to use the Scriptures, to live in relationship, and to administer the church's corporate life, including evangelism and nurture. Development of skill in churchmanship is more than technique. It is God reaching out to man so that man might perceive his need and accept God's gift of himself. Accordingly, the Christian educators studied are not content with learning that issues in proficiency alone. Proficiency is only a servant in the communication of the gospel. Unless this is clearly understood, there is no basis for a responsible evaluation of learning theory's ability to account for, and to predict, the skill-habit concerns of Christian nurture.

Because the church is a worshiping community, persons committed to its care must learn the skills and habits of the devotional life. In one sense, worship is itself educational. We do learn to worship as we participate in the corporate praise of God. For some, there may be "apprehension without full comprehension," [28] but this is no substitute for a conscious attempt to experience growth in the techniques of private, family, and congregational worship. The roles of the group participant and the worship leader are different in function rather than essence. No leader can destroy the validity of worship, but he may be so lacking in the skill of Scripture-reading and public prayer, for example, that he becomes a hindrance rather than a help. Control of the voice, the use of pauses, gestures, and eye contact are all significant aspects of leadership in worship. This is not to say that Christian nurture is satisfied when the mechanics of reading are learned. How one reads is also dependent upon a personal conception of God and the theological meaning of the passage to be read. Dietrich Bonhoeffer has cautioned against any easy optimism that equates vocal proficiency in Scripture-reading with depth of worship. "I shall be able . . . to express the fact that it is God who is angered, who is consoling and admonishing, not by indifferent monotony, but only with inmost concern and rapport, as one who knows that he himself is being addressed. It will make all the difference between right and wrong reading of Scriptures if I do not identify myself with God but quite simply serve him." [29] Surely the skill-habits of the devotional life are to be considered integral with the nature of the church.

If skill in worship is a necessity to realize the fullest potential of our relationship with God, skill is also required for living in relationship with members of the Christian community. By virtue of our election in Jesus Christ, we are already in community. Therefore, from one perspective, living in relationship is a gift of God. It is not a human achievement. From another view, living in relationship as members of the body of Christ requires skills as the result of learning. To recapitulate, the Christian community is God's decision, but lack of experience in expressing the community may cause the nature of the church to be eclipsed. It is still present but now hidden because persons have not learned skills in face-to-face encounter as members of the church. Christian nurture anticipates that skills of group process be attained not that the individual may be handled by either the leader or the group but that persons may learn to communicate with one another.[30]

To live in relationship with other people requires facility in mastering the art of listening, willingness to assume the responsibility demanded by the situation, and skill in observing the dynamics of the fellowship in study. Living in relationship is the attempt to learn how to be the redemptive community in all circumstances. Unless Christians develop skill in handling the different interpersonal situations of the church's life, the cutting edge of its message is made dull. If Christians encounter overwhelming problems in dealing with one another, why should others become excited about giving themselves in obedience to Christ? Florence Allshorn's St. Julian's home for returned missionaries grew out of a desire to learn the skills of corporate Christian life. "Those who learned to live in daily, growing, wholehearted response to the two great realities of man's life, God and neighbor, became really free persons." [31] Something similar is involved in the interdenominational experiment at Stony Point, New York, for the orientation of new fraternal workers. Candidates spend a period of five months together in worship, study, and work, developing skills of the corporate life. The Stony Point venture cannot be duplicated by local congregations, but the skill-habits of living in relationship remain concerns to be learned in Christian nurture. The truth is that most churches have failed miserably at this point. They have learned how to be busy, but they have not learned how to implement that quality of corporate living that reflects the full orb of the gospel.

Christian educators are also determined that persons learn the skills of churchmanship. At a minimum, this implies skill in thinking about and administering the church as an organization. Vieth stated this as an objective of religious education in 1930: " To develop in growing persons the ability and disposition to participate in the organized society of Christians — the church." [32] Today this concern may seem obvious, but it has not always been so. Until about 1922 when the International Council of Religious Education was founded, Christian nurture was carried on by lay movements independent of denominational direction. Persons received Biblical instruction, but religion was essentially a private affair. This was admirably suited to the individualistic temperament of the frontier. However, it did not result in the communication of the organismic character of the church. It was implied that personal salvation was everything, but the nurturing community into which the new Christian entered was of relatively lesser importance. Christian nurture has had to face how the individual will express his relationship to the church and how the church will objectify its relationship to individuals. Unless there is careful attention given to learning to be churchmen, a schism may develop between the church's nature and its expression in the world. In this case, administration may become a detriment to the gospel. It would be better if there were no organization. But where time is taken to think seriously about the kind of administration demanded by the nature of the church and the need of the contemporaneous situation, structure can be a vehicle for hearing God speak.[33] The Presbyterian penchant for things being done " decently and in order " is more than a quirk of denominational pride. It is a way to express a quality of administration shared by the ecumenical church. Learning the skills of churchmanship does not solve all problems of the church. Nevertheless, neither are these problems solved by disorder. Miller writes: "A properly organized congregation, administered in terms of objectives that are clearly formulated, is more likely to achieve that quality of life whereby Christian education will be the experience of every member than will a congregation organized for the tastes of a few individuals, or for the adults only, or for children only." [34] Churchmanship is a skill that does not happen by itself. It must be learned.

## Motives

Educators have long considered the problem of discovering the proper motivation as the key to learning. If only the proper motivation could be aroused, learning would follow as a necessary consequence. The purpose of the teacher would then be to provide guidance to the student in order to utilize his learning potential. In practice, however, teachers of required subjects, especially, often spend their time trying to devise novel ways of stimulating students to want to learn rather than to be able to teach on the basis of motivation already present.

Secular studies in learning theory usually presume that the stimulus for learning is the result of deficit motivation. This means that organisms learn in order to reduce tensions arising from hunger, thirst, anxiety, fear, and the threat of insecurity. This is avoidance learning. There is no doubt that this is true. Persons do not escape from their biological relationship with other organisms. They are actuated to move toward equilibrium. Yet, when this is stated there is an element of learning which is being neglected.

Christian nurture focuses on motives that go beyond avoidance learning. As internal triggers for action, motives cannot be accepted as they are. They are in need of reconstruction. There must be a development of motives which are in tension with those which seek to meet a felt need.

This is the case, as Nels Ferré has said, because "adjustment to the environment in its actual behavior leaves us exactly where we are — in trouble and in need of help!"[35] The revelation of God in Jesus Christ indicates that the Christian can be content with nothing less than a willingness to go against the safety implicit in deficit motivation.

The Christian is called to live as God's representative in the world. This is the broad outline of mission. But when attention is given to concrete attempts to fulfill the commission, questions of motivation arise. Action in Christ's name may be undertaken to satisfy some deficiency in the person's character or as atonement for unresolved guilt rather than because the encounter with God requires it as the compulsion of faith. The end is good, but the motivation is unacceptable. Christian nurture desires the learned motive best described as discipleship.

Instead of deficit motivation, there is the disposition to choose actions which may violate every expectation for comfort and self-preservation. Jesus called twelve men to follow him, but motivation consistent with this new relationship happened only after the trauma of learning in depth. An indication of this is given when after nearly three years, James and John were thinking of their call in terms of preferential positions. This was nothing less than deficit-motivated-action based on a concern for self-enhancement. (Mark 10:35-45.) Yet in patience Jesus taught that basic motivation could only be hindered by concentrating upon personal needs. "If any man would come after me, let him deny himself and take up his cross and follow me. For whoever would save his life will lose it, and whoever loses his life for my sake will find it." (Matt. 16:24b-25.) The picture is that of a condemned man triumphing over his executioners. This is discipleship. It may result in misunderstanding, ostracism, suffering, and even death. Nevertheless, the Christian learns to shunt aside all lesser motives than discipleship of Jesus Christ. In a word, discipleship as a motive has to do with being ready to express what it means to be enlisted, mobilized, and deployed for Christ's sake with a sensitivity for the cost that may be involved.

Obedience to God is another learned motive for Christian action. It is the way the Christian orders his life. Viewed objectively, many acts deserve the judgment of approval in the market place of values. But the " why " of a person's conduct is as important as the " what." It is good to alleviate human suffering as a confession of human solidarity. As a person, the neighbor has a claim on my ministry. Yet when one becomes yoked with Christ, the neighbor's claim is caught up in the larger context of living under orders of the King of Kings and Lord of Lords. In its attempt to develop this kind of motivation, Christian nurture doubtless fails many times. However, the failure only calls to attention the greater need to consider obedience to Jesus Christ as the motivation for acts of devotion. The question of vocation must also be resolved with reference to the motivation of the claim of God. Young persons especially need to analyze their motives in choosing a lifework. The vocation may be a commendable one, but Christian nurture challenges the individual to re-examine his motives to see whether they reflect the cultural values or the desire for obedience. The disciple is not greater than his Master, and the Master learned obedience!

A further suggestive insight for motives as a concern to be learned is pointed up by the word " repentance." Its root meaning is a changed mind. Through confrontation with the gospel, persons may be led to repentance out of fear of damnation. A genuine fear may have a place in the initial encounter. But if this is the basis for learning to repent of one's continued involvement in sin, fear of damnation is similar to the avoidance learning of some secular theories. In contrast, Christian nurture accepts the seriousness of sin and the necessity for repentance. It is held that the steadfastness of God's mercy is the authentic learned motive for repentance.

In brief, motives are significant for learning in Christian nurture, but they are also the result of learning.

## Changes in the Self

Before it is fruitful to describe " change in the self " as a concern to be learned, attention should be turned to what is understood by the term " self." [36] A definition of the self is apt to be mercurial in character. Just as soon as we think it has been made known, it is likely to slip from our grasp.

With this risk in mind, the self is defined as the structural totality of the individual person formed through interaction with the not-self world, other selves, and the Self who is God. There is no suggestion of a disembodied super-control substance beyond mind and body. Neither is the definition content to consider selfhood as existing either in the purely biological or the psychological realms. There is a dimension of selfhood which cannot be described except in relationship to the God who is.[37] As Albert Outler has emphasized, the Christian view of self is radically theocentric: " man from God, man before God, man against God, man redeemed by God, man in communion with God, in and through the God-man." [38] Consequently, selfhood is not limited to the present life. Maintaining its identity, it transcends death.

The view of the self just outlined finds the concept of gestalt congenial. Selfhood involves a structural pattern as well as a restructuring of impressions from without and reorganization from within that results in various structures now becoming figure while others recede into ground. At another moment, the current ground may become figure.[39] The structures constituting the self such as body, mind, and spirit may be described, but the self is more than the sum of the total structures. The self is a unity, even as Risieri Frondizi has written, " formed upon substructures and the intimate and complex interrelations of these substructures." [40] To describe man as a self is to acknowledge that he is a whole: body, mind, and spirit. Any emphasis upon the one to the detriment of the others results in brokenness of the self.

Selfhood is always dynamic. It is in a process of becoming unless hindered by disease or injury. For this reason, Christian nurture takes seriously its participatory role in guiding the quality of that becoming. There is always change in the self regardless of how the self is understood. But if the individual really is not a self apart from relationship with God, then any secularist description of becoming is unable to do full justice to the radical nature of selfhood. There must be nurture which corresponds with the self's nature. This includes the present self as well as the potential self. The present self is the individual as he now is in various states of brokenness. The potential self is what he is as God anticipates him to be. Stated in terms of a concern to be learned, Christian becoming must include fundamental changes in the self that go beyond changes as the result of such concerns as knowledge and understanding.

Change in the self is related to each of the previous concerns largely through its priority. Unless this crucial learning has occurred, that transformation of self as intended by God in the death and resurrection of Jesus Christ is absent. It is admitted that change in the self is hardly a precise term, but it is useful to point to the deep learning known where persons have a genuine relationship with God, where they have been confronted by him, know it, and under his power respond affirmatively. It is the one concern to be learned which determines whether there has been Christian nurture leading to commitment or only to general learning.

Change in the self is not a once-for-all event. It has the overtones of conversion but is distinct from it. Conversion is the initial confession of faith. Yet it is not enough to be continually looking backward to the moment when Christ became personally relevant. This is only the beginning for the sometimes discouraging and other times thrilling experience of learning implications of the initial conversion. Christian nurture presupposes continued change in the self under the Holy Spirit.

This study necessitates the difficult juxtaposition of three separate disciplines: Christian education theory, learning theory, and Christian theology. But before it can be profitable to bring them into relationship, they must be investigated separately.

From the side of Christian education, it is now clear what demands are made upon learning theory. These have been described as seven concerns to be learned. For the present, nothing more is to be done with them. When the time comes to evaluate the theological integrity of learning theory as theory and as it offers solutions to the concerns to be learned, only one expression of the latter will be used. For example, instead of dealing with the broad aspects of knowledge discussed, God's mighty acts in Israel's history may be considered a representative knowledge problem. A similar procedure will be in effect for each of the other six concerns to be learned.

Attention is now directed to the nature of four theories of learning as these present their claims to be adequate for all types of human becoming, including Christian nurture.

## CHAPTER III

# Representative Theories of Learning

IN SPITE of the plethora of reports on learning-theory research appearing in such professional journals as *The Psychological Review* and *The Journal of Experimental Psychology,* learning theory has been largely unproductive in giving help to educators.[1] Educational procedures and learning theory seem to move along parallel lines without coming into relationship. Donald Snygg contends that "the practices of the typical school have remained completely unaffected by any learning theory of the last thirty-five years." [2] Although learning theorists would not describe the situation in quite the same terms, they would acknowledge that educators ought not to expect concrete help from learning theory. William K. Estes writes, "We find no rational grounds for expecting direct transfer of laboratory findings or direct application of basic psychological theories to problems of the schoolroom." [3] It is held that the relation between education and learning theory is more like physiology to medicine than medicine to the patient.

Where does this leave the educator? Two main positions are open to him. Since he is primarily concerned with modifying human rather than subhuman behavior, the temptation to completely ignore learning theorists, with their mazes and puzzle boxes, and go on to relevant research for the classroom is obviously present. This approach does not reflect the seriousness which the problem demands.

Procedure ought to be grounded in the fundamental way learning is judged to take place. Without the basic learning theory, there may be practice without a dependable referent.

A second approach to the problem becomes a matter of interpreting various learning theories according to their adequacy in meeting problems of educational theory and practice. The needs of education determine the kinds of questions the theory must answer.[4] It is admitted that this procedure does not find much support from learning theorists. Estes goes on to write that laboratory-based theories cannot be tested in the classroom. Theories are rendered valid or invalid only with regard to the conditions which satisfy the assumptions of the experiment.[5] This position is technically true. However, a learning theory that is indifferent to the concerns found in educational theory and practice runs the risk of becoming an experimental dilettantism. Then learning theory loses its appeal as a partner with education seeking to understand the way to a modification of human behavior. As Snygg has said perhaps with tongue in cheek, learning theorists may make "rather good professional careers out of attacking the weak points in one another's theories, much like the shipwrecked Scotsmen who made a good living by taking in one another's washing."[6]

The second approach is to be commended. It is assumed that learning theories provide basic information about the learning process even though no single theory may encompass all the experimental data. This requires an attempt to come to an understanding of the nuclear structure of a particular learning theory without becoming involved in the total ramifications of the theory.

The four principal theories — reinforcement, conditioning, gestalt, and sign-gestalt — will be sketched according to their root formulations. An assessment of the strengths and weaknesses of the individual theories will follow by drawing upon secondary learning-theory sources, related psychological studies, anthropological insights, and personal restructuring of the existing data. This task will not be limited to experimental data. While this plan makes no claim to being scientific, it may provide resources for a handling of the current experimental impasse. There is a precedent for this analysis of the problem as is evident in the thesis of Arthur Combs and Donald Snygg. After acknowledging that there are difficulties in accepting subjective facts as relevant for scientific purposes, they nevertheless maintain that these facts cannot be disregarded just because they are difficult to measure. " If behavior is a function of perception, then a science of human relationships must concern itself with the meaning of events for the behaver as well as for the observer. Human feelings, attitudes, fears, hopes, wants, likes, and aversions cannot be set aside while we deal with objective events." [7] Abraham Maslow, too, holds to the validity of nonobjective data when dealing with human behavior. In his remarks before the Nebraska Symposium on Motivation, he states that he is not just a seeker after " cold " facts. He is concerned with man's fate, ends, goals, and future.[8]

## Reinforcement Theory

The literature of learning theory provides almost innumerable reports on experiments designed to gain knowledge of some aspects of the learning process. However, within this mass of material, in spite of differences in detail, types of experiments emerge for each theory which may justly be designated as " classical." The latter term is used because so much research is based either implicitly or explicitly upon these basic experiments. These reports are useful for introducing the theory and for providing a referent for learning-theory language.

In reinforcement theory, the experiment is so designed that the subject, usually a white rat, can solve the problem only by running off a series of incorrect or unproductive movements until one happens to be correct. The random actions of the subject result in its accidentally bumping a protruding lever which activates a food-pellet mechanism that drops a pellet in the food receptacle. When the animal eats the food, the movement has been rewarded. The pressing of the lever has been *reinforced.* On subsequent trials, there is a tendency to engage in fewer trial-and-error movements. When the lever is pressed immediately upon being introduced to the experimental box, the animal has learned the problem. A habit has been formed. Should food not be available, the subject will continue to press the lever for a time. Since the movement is not reinforced, the lever-pressing habit tends to become extinct.

Before the subject in the classical experiment can receive any reward, it must be in motion. A food-satiated rat may go to sleep. Therefore, there is no motion, no reward, and no learning. Thorndike calls this disposition for action the " law of readiness." [9] The tendency to repeat an action that was satisfying and to avoid the unsatisfactory state of affairs is called the " law of effect." [10] Clark Hull describes trial-and-error learning with reinforcement substantially as does Thorndike: " Simple trial-and-error learning . . . takes place in normal mammalian organisms when they are presented with a stimulus situation that either through the organism's inheritance or previous learning, or both, tends to evoke two or more distinguishable reactions, of which only one receives reinforcement. In case the competing reaction potentials are two, and both are weak but equal in strength, there will be first a more or less irregular alternation between them, the erroneous one gradually becoming weakened by experimental extinction and the successful one being strengthened by reinforcement." [11] Experimental extinction refers to the likelihood of a response becoming weakened in the absence of reward.

The disposition to do what was rewarding in a previous situation permits prediction of what an organism is likely to do under similar circumstances. When the reward is an answer to basic needs such as hunger, it is known as primary reinforcement.

Hull recognizes that not all reinforcement is of the all-or-none variety of the primary type. Reinforcement, especially in higher mental processes, follows a "gradient of reinforcement." This postulate states that in a series of acts, the acts which are closest to the reward will be reinforced to a greater degree than those farthest from the goal. The primary need is not ultimately satisfied by the rat's sniffing at the bar press in the classical experiment, but the animal is closer to realizing the food than when it was at the opposite end of the box. Sniffing in this experiment is a form of " secondary reinforcement." Hull explains it as an " increasing function of the approximation to the conditions necessary to primary reinforcement." [12]

In archery practice, the stance, the position of the arrow in the bow, and the tension applied to the bow will receive primary reinforcement if they result in hitting the center of the target. Falling short of the central target, there will be greater reinforcement if the arrow hits the side of the target than if it overshoots the target completely. This reinforcement and others of similar nature are all secondary, but they facilitate learning and therefore function as a primary reward.

Miller and Dollard, too, consider all learning to be of the reinforcement type. Useful inventions and improvement of cultural habits may have made their appearance at an earlier point in history, but they did not occur. They could not be rewarded and did not become part of the cultural heritage. If a response must occur before it can be rewarded, the foundational task of teaching is " to arrange the situation so that the learner will somehow make the first correct response." [13] When the correct response has been elicited, it may be rewarded and learned.

Four elements enter into all learning. The learner must be motivated. He must be able to discriminate the one correct or cluster of correct stimuli cues from a host of cues. He must actively make some response whether this is rewarded or not. Finally, the learner must be rewarded if the desired response is achieved.[14] If responses must always occur before they can be rewarded, what novelty is added by learning? "The new feature is that the particular response rewarded now occurs regularly to a specific cue, whereas previously its occurrence at just that time and place may have been exceedingly infrequent. The connection between cue and response is the new product of learning."[15]

In human learning, once the appropriate response and cues are brought together, language may become of assistance in correlating responses and drive.[16] Language becomes utilized as a short cut to the usual trial-and-error method. The learner thinks through a series of possible responses without overt action. When a response pattern appears plausible, it may be tested. If it is correct and is rewarded, learning will have occurred.

## Conditioning Theory

Four terms are used in conditioning experiments: The *unconditioned stimulus* elicits the initial response of the organism. The *unconditioned response* is the response made to the unconditioned stimulus. The *conditioned stimulus* is a neutral stimulus that becomes connected with the unconditioned stimulus in ability to elicit responses. The *conditioned response* is the new response that is now made in the presence of the conditioned stimulus alone.

In conditioning experiments, a box is designed with a barrier dividing the floor area into two compartments. The floor on one side of the barrier contains a grid that may be electrified by the operator. A buzzer set on the wall of the box may be activated by the experimenter or correlated automatically with the onset of shock.

An animal, usually a white rat, is placed on the grid side of the compartment. The learning task is to jump the barrier. When the current (unconditioned stimulus) is turned on, the rat is greatly discomfited. It eventually jumps the barrier and escapes from shock. When this pattern has become established, the buzzer (conditioned stimulus) is sounded just prior to shock. Now the rat learns to jump the barrier on cue of the buzzer and without the stimulus of shock. There has been conditioning to the sound of the buzzer. The animal has learned.

Although there are varieties of conditioning theory, that of E. R. Guthrie will be used as representative because he has achieved a sophisticated system through reducing all learning to conditioning.[17] Other theorists who hold to conditioning postulates often drift into a variation of reinforcement theory. Guthrie is a " purist " in terms of conditioning.

His orientation is behavioristic. He is not interested in evidence from the subject's internal frame of reference because it is not controlled. For him, theory must be developed on the basis of controlled situations in order to predict an organism's actions. Ultimately, however, Guthrie is more interested in what a person does in complex learning situations than in what frenzied rats may do in a laboratory box. Even though behaviorism is accused of forgetting the main actor, the man himself, Guthrie asserts that this is less than accurate. The man may be taken too much for granted, but he is not denied.[18] His theory is often illustrated with rather delightful incidents from human experiences. For example, he relates the story of the country parson whose horse became victim of reverse conditioning. While the minister was calling on the parents, the small boys had the minister's horse in the barn. One boy would yell, " whoa " while the other would jab the animal with a pitchfork. Needless to say, the pastor had some difficult moments when he tried to manage his horse without knowing the cause of the usually gentle beast's strange actions!

Although his interests are in what persons may be predicted to do, he must go back to the classical experiment on conditioning. He holds that the relationships in conditioning are often misunderstood. Instead of measuring the time interval between the unconditioned stimulus (shock) and the conditioned stimulus (buzzer), the basic relationship is the *time* between the conditioned stimulus and the conditioned response. "It is not the two stimuli that are associated, but the substitute cue and the resultant act."[19] What the learner does is what he learns. "Whether a student will be able to read in the bustle of a library room depends on his early experiences there. If he begins with an engrossing book, he will attain quick adaptation to the noise about him. If he begins by noticing what is going on in the room, the open book will eventually be a mere cue for looking about."[20]

While learning takes place in a single combination of conditioned stimulus and response, the actual conditioned stimulus may be different from the one usually discerned. The true conditioning stimulus in the classical experiment is not the buzzer. The true conditioners are the nerve cells of the peripheral nervous system. These issue in some type of movement. "Every such motion is a stimulus to many sense organs in muscles, tendons, and joints, as well as the occasion for changing stimuli to eyes, ears, etc. We may call them *movement-produced* stimuli, for the reason that they are produced by our own movements."[21]

The mechanism of movement-produced stimuli permits wide application of conditioned responses. Skills are learned through association of many cues and responses. A skill is a system of habits organized for some specific result. In time, some irrelevant movements are dropped until essential cues are correlated with the necessary responses. Repetition does not improve performance in the sense of increasing learning. All learning occurs in the one relationship between conditioned stimulus and response. Repetition provides thousands of habit responses attached to proper cues. The more complex the skill, the more numerous are the specific cues and responses to be learned.

The learning of intellectual skills is held to be no different from any other skill. Playing chess and playing tennis are learned in the same way. Just as there are movements in physical skills, so there are movements involved in intellectual skills. It is contended that movements are associated in thought itself. This is valid, according to Guthrie, because no one can think a sentence without developing tension in the muscles used in speech. " It is my belief . . . that all thought trains depend on movement trains, and that in all instances the association of ideas is an association of successive movements through conditioning." [22]

The basic contribution of Guthrie is his plausible account of all learning as one trial contiguous conditioning. Whether the learning is " thinking " or " doing," conditioning is held to be adequate explanation.

## Gestalt Theory

Gestalt theory, as the German word implies, has to do with " form " and primarily the perception of form. This is understood as a function of organization. With the perceptual interest as a point of departure, gestalt theory has been widened to include implications for learning as well as personality theory.

Two types of experiments are illustrative of the gestalt research: perceptual, and *Umwege,* roundabout or detour. In perceptual experiments, certain figures are presented to human subjects. These may be line drawings with hidden letters. The problem is to determine if the subject can perceive the hidden letters without being told that he is to look for the letters in the figure. Not until the subject is directed to search for the particular letters are they likely to be perceived. Instead of a stimulus-response explanation as in reinforcement theory, gestaltists say that the instruction has helped the subject restructure the perceived field.[23]

In the typical *Umwege* experiment, there is an open barrier between the organism and the food or goal object. If the barrier is not continuous, the problem for the subject is to perceive the relationship of the path around the barrier without trial and error. If the barrier is continuous, the problem is modified. The food is beyond reach of the experimental organism. Yet resources are available to the organism to obtain the goal food if they are utilized in the proper manner. Two short, hollow sticks are in the enclosure with the subject. After studying the food and giving evidence of annoyance at being unable to get the food, the animal may suddenly fit the two hollow sticks together forming a tool. With this tool, it is able to push the food within reach. Instead of trial and error, there appears to be evidence of insight, the sudden realization that the sticks might be used as a useful instrument. Wolfgang Köhler has analyzed the meaning of this familiar experiment with the chimpanzee, Sultan, as an indication of insight over trial-and-error learning. "An insightful treatment of the material offered in the training series is one governed by an apprehension of the structural principle of that material. . . . Sultan's insight consisted in his recognizing that this [fitting two different-sized sticks together] difference depended upon the relative size of the two sticks. His behavior could not be called insightful if success in fitting the sticks together had come as a result of fumbling with them. It was insightful if he *saw* which stick could be thrust into the other." [24] Charles Osgood defines certain principles for learning on the basis of this experiment. (*a*) Insight is more likely to occur if the goal tension is more moderate than excessive. In this case, the subject may be "frozen" to the spot in front of the goal without being able to see the necessary relationship of the goal and the way "around" the barrier through the development of the appropriate tool. (*b*) To the extent that the organism varies its position in the geographical field, reorganization is facilitated. (*c*) The less distance between the goal and a tool in the psychological field, the more likely insightful organization or restructuring is to occur.[25]

The dynamic of gestalt theory is related to the " law of *Prägnanz*." K. Koffka affirms Wertheimer's description of *Prägnanz* as being substantially correct. " It can briefly be formulated like this: psychological organization will always be as ' good ' as the prevailing conditions allow. In this definition, the term ' good ' is undefined. It embraces such properties as regularity, symmetry, simplicity." [26] *Prägnanz* has to do with a tendency in the organism to produce the most symmetrical and meaningful whole. Closure is an expression of the tendency toward wholeness. For example, three lines arranged in the shape of a triangle but which do not actually touch one another are perceived as a triangle. Strictly speaking, there is no " figure." There are only three lines arranged in a familiar way. The mind fills in the " gaps." This happens, too, when we hear a speaker who is not at home in our language. For a brief moment, his mispronounced words are disturbing, but very soon the words are understood in terms of their meaning to such a degree that the errors are no longer noticed. David Katz reasons that Newton and Galileo were successful in their formulations of the respective laws of gravity and the pendulum because their efforts resulted in mental tension. " In each instance the mental gap called for closure, and what the scientists observed just fitted into the gap like the last piece of a puzzle." [27]

The gestalt orientation is more interested in understanding how complex phenomena may be related meaningfully than in talking about stimuli and responses becoming connected. This does not mean that stimuli and responses are of no concern. They are viewed as subordinate rather than primary foci of attention. Instead of concentration upon rigid stimulus-response connections, there is emphasis upon field organization, the relationship of parts and wholes as these are organized by the perceiving individuals.

As an illustration of field organization, Koffka observes that two " taps " may be heard as a unity. The first tap, temporally speaking, has ceased to exist when the second tap is sounded. Yet they are heard as a pair.[28] This suggests that structure is significant for learning even as Jerome Bruner has indicated. " Grasping the structure of a subject is understanding it in a way that permits many other things to be related to it meaningfully. To learn structure, in short, is to learn how things are related." [29]

Unlike most learning theorists, Koffka considers the ego, or self concept, a necessity.[30] The use of ego-involvement in field organization can be expected to result in meaningful learning. Whereas stimulus-response reinforcement and conditioning theorists do not appear to be concerned about the organism's own activities in being selective about stimuli to which it will respond, gestaltists are at their best when dealing with meaningful relations. Furthermore, gestalt theorists do not think that judgments of the self are less than scientific. Self-analysis is a means to discover processes that defy the efforts of animal psychologists.[31]

In brief, given the mental capacity, tools to be utilized, and to a certain extent, past experience, organisms may be expected to find correct solutions through the mechanism of reorganization of the perceived field. This is done with a minimum of movement. If a variety of responses is tried, the various responses become hypotheses to be tested. Humanly speaking, the organism in the classical experiment " understood " what it was doing in relationship to the needs of the situation. For this reason, the wider implications of seeing relationships mean that productive thinking involves the structuring of the problem by the self and of structuring the problem under guidance. This is the essence of learning.

## Sign-Gestalt Theory

The classical sign-gestalt experiment is a simplified maze with an entrance and a food receptacle at the end point.[32] Two groups of rats are used in the experiment. The control animals are placed in the maze at the entrance and are fed when they reach the food area. This procedure is followed for several days. Up until this point, the experiment corresponds to the stimulus-response reinforcement type.

In the sign-gestalt test, the noncontrol rats are given access to the maze but without reinforcement of food. They roam through the maze including the place where the food will be placed. When food is introduced, the performance abruptly becomes like that of the control animals. Theorists such as Edward Tolman say that the previously nonrewarded organisms are learning " expectancies." Not only are they learning to avoid " dead ends," but they are also learning continuing pathways to the goal. Tolman rejects an explanation of stamping in of stimulus-response habits as doing justice to the evidence. " The presence of reinforcement in a particular locus makes that locus a goal which determines what performance will take place, but it does not stamp in S–R connections though it probably does give a special vividness to that locus in the field expectancy." [33]

Tolman's sign learning is characterized as purposive. But this has nothing to do with purpose in metaphysics. It is the purpose observed in animals seeking to reach a certain goal. The development of preferred patterns to the goal implies cognitions. The animal " knows " where it is going. It is not stumbling as a matter of trial and error.

Sign-gestalt theory is understood to be molar, that is, it has properties of its own other than those of the underlying physics and physiology. The distinctive properties of molar behavior are at least three in number: Behavior has the sense of getting-to or getting-from a specific goal-object or goal-situation. The rat in the maze is getting to food. Behavior always involves a mutual exchange between a behavior-act and the environment. The rat's getting to food expresses itself in a specific pattern of running, and choosing some alleys rather than others. Behavior is characterized in terms of greater readiness for short or easy-means activities than long ones.

In Tolman's vocabulary, these elements of molar behavior are known respectively as significate, sign, and significate-means-ends relations. Together, they form a sign-gestalt, the total learning situation of the moment. Since behavior is purposive, it moves forward in expectation of a goal. Learning is the building up of sign-gestalt expectations.

Tolman lists three " moods " of these expectancies as perceptions, mnemonization (memory), and inferences. In a *perceptual* sign-gestalt, stimuli corresponding to all parts of the sign-gestalt are present. All elements needed for the solution are at hand. Past experience is at a minimum. In *mnemonization,* stimuli for the distinctive features of the maze (sign) only are present. The organism does not know that the desired food (significate) is actually in the goal area. Neither does it know the most direct route to the goal (significate-means-end). Yet it has had specific past experiences in the maze and through memory completes the sign-gestalt of the whole situation. In the *inference* mood, again stimuli for the sign only are present. Stimuli for the significate and means-end relations are absent for this particular maze. There has been experience with other mazes. Therefore, present stimuli and generalized past experience, by inference, become a new sign-gestalt leading to the solution.[34]

The classical sign-gestalt experiment is basic to Tolman's theory. To the casual observer, the subject is engaging in purposeless behavior. But it is actually developing sign-gestalt expectations through examining where food is not and where it may likely be. It is acquiring " cognitive maps " of the entire maze or learning situation. It is actively engaged in learning. " Learning requires first a differentiation between the *this* which leads on, and the *that* which does not lead on; and *then,* . . . further integration of the succession of these ' thises ' into an extensive ' this.' " [35]

## Strengths and Weaknesses of the Four Theories

### *Reinforcement Theory*

1. Strengths

The most obvious strength of reinforcement theory is its commonsense appeal. From time immemorial, parents have used rewards to develop acceptable behavior and punishments to discourage nonconformity. We do find learning more enjoyable when we feel we are making some progress. Miller and Dollard relate the experience of a boy trying to learn to play the piano. When he had learned his fingering, he was told his timing was off or his expression was poor, but never did the boy hear an encouraging word. The only action rewarded was escape from an anxiety-inducing situation. Consequently, the boy failed to learn to play the piano.[36]

The structure of reinforcement theory has been found useful to describe conditions discerned in anthropological investigations. To find such support in a nonpsychological discipline is an obvious strength. Theodore Brameld paraphrases this view: " Culture provides both the conscious and unconscious conditions for learning. . . . Culture encompasses certain conscious and unconscious responses and discourages others, depending in turn upon habits previously established. . . . Culture reinforces these responses by systems of reward and punishment, and . . . culture tends to perpetuate itself by means of the learning that thus occurs." [37] Clyde Kluckhohn accepts the reinforcement postulate too, as the *sine qua non* of learning. " In every culture . . . success or reward is essential to all learning. If a response is not rewarded, it will not be learned." [38] Culture determines the kind and quality of the reward. It specifies the value judgments of " good " and " bad." Accordingly, culturally approved habits become learned to the extent that the action is rewarded. Culture need not punish the learner for nonconformist behavior. It merely withholds the reward. Therefore, cultural learning operates on the principle of extinction rather than punishment.[39]

So-called " teaching machines " are based in part on the reinforcement principle. These differ in detail, but they are alike in arranging the learning material in ascending degrees of complexity. At each stage, the student writes the answer and then checks it immediately with the " key." Instead of waiting until the evaluation is received from the teacher, the student is rewarded or punished directly. As the components of a learning task become isolated and learned, the total result becomes a gradual increment in knowledge. At each step along the way, the learner is given opportunity to find satisfaction in what he is achieving. Reinforcement theory reminds teachers that too-difficult tasks may increase the sense of failure and hence, inhibit learning. Tasks must be chosen where the possibility of learning success is at an optimum.

Of all the theories of learning, reinforcement commands the allegiance of more theorists than any other theory. This fact must be taken seriously. It has developed more experiments than other theories and has attempted to meet the objections of its critics.[40]

Hull has made a cogent defense of reinforcement theory's ability to deal with the experimental evidence of conditioning. The problem is this: If learning occurs only through reinforcement, how can a neutral stimulus be given power to evoke the avoidance reaction? Reinforcement theory would be adequate to account for proficiency in leaping the barrier in the classical conditioning experiment, but the rat would need to experience the pain of shock first. There is no pain connected with the buzzer, consequently there can be no reward in escaping. Hull posits secondary reinforcement as a way out of the dilemma. The sound of the buzzer itself becomes a reward signifying escape from pain. Hence, in the future, whenever the buzzer is heard, the animal will leap the barrier.[41]

He understands higher mental processes in man as due to the mechanism of the fractional antedating goal response. This is defined as a response "evoked earlier in the stimulus sequence than the point corresponding to the circumstances of its original reinforcement." [42] In terms of the classical condition experiment, the learner comes to anticipate the shock when the buzzer sounds. The response of jumping the barrier is moved up or antedates the onset of shock. Hull contends that this same mechanism operates when man expresses acts described as foresightful or expectative.[43]

In man, the fractional antedating goal response produces other stimuli which have no instrumental value but to guide behavior. These pure stimulus acts are the basis for ideas.[44] These become stimuli for other responses. Insight, the spontaneous bringing together of two elements not previously related in closeness of association, is explained through the same process. Previously rewarded stimulus-response experiences are moved forward in time to shorten the normal trial-and-error behavior expected without insight. Reference is made to an experiment with apes that had an opportunity to engage in playful activity with sticks. When food was placed beyond reach of the apes, the ones engaging in play combined the sticks at once to form a food-reaching instrument. Insight was a function of the instrument-using habit.[45] It is generalized that insight in man is not due to some mysterious faculty but to a recombination of previous habits, learnings.

Miller and Dollard discuss reasoning as due to longer sequences of cue-producing responses with reinforcement. However, primary rewards and punishments are not administered directly in the trial-and-error ventures of thinking. The mental responses become accepted or rejected in terms of their acquired reward or acquired anxiety value of the produced cue. If the cue is associated with reward, the connection tends to be strengthened. If the cue becomes connected with anxiety-produced responses, the connection is weakened and will likely be abandoned. In other words, the function of reasoning and insight is to produce initial responses. " Once produced, the responses are all subject to the same laws of trial-and-error learning, to rejection or selection on the basis of the effects of nonreward or reward." [46]

The contribution of reinforcement is an impressive one. There is small wonder that it provides a formidable challenge to all other theories.

2. Weaknesses

If there are strengths in reinforcement theory, there are also significant weaknesses.

A basic weakness is the attempt to account for all learning on the one principle of reinforcement. It will become evident that the law of effect cannot support the weight which it must carry in reinforcement theory. Harry Harlow has carried out a series of experiments on the manipulation or exploration drives in monkeys. The subjects are able to solve both simple and complex problems with no other reward than the satisfaction of curiosity itself. Furthermore, no evidence exists that hunger-appetite or anxiety-avoidance systems are the foundations of curiosity or vice versa. There is interaction but not dependence. " At best anxiety is a motive for avoidant behavior, and the greatest part of human motivation is positive searching toward goals, not mere avoidance." [47]

Maslow, who has studied the *well* person rather than the sick, is equally critical of reinforcement theory. He asserts that there are two basic types of motives: deficit and growth. Reinforcement theory builds its postulates on deficit motivation, but this represents only a minor part of the total learning experience of man. Because reinforcement learning theory has been so preoccupied with deficit motives, it is appropriate for a very limited body of knowledge.[48]

Man and his learning experiences, according to Maslow, can best be understood by concentrating upon him as dominated by growth motives. "When we examine people who are predominantly growth-motivated, the coming-to-rest conception of motivation becomes completely useless. In such people, gratification breeds increased rather than decreased motivation, heightened rather than lessened excitement." [49] The person as person cannot be the stimulus-response man set into motion by external stimuli. Healthy persons are not essentially reactive. They are self-actualizing and self-determining. "The determinants which govern them are now primarily inner ones, rather than social or environmental. They are the laws of their own inner nature, their potentialities and capacities, their talents, their latent resources, their creative impulses, their needs to know themselves and to become more and more integrated and unified, more and more aware of what they really are, of what they really want." [50] Maslow concludes categorically that the highest possible development in human relationships cannot base itself on a deficit theory of motivation as in reinforcement theory.[51]

Gordon Allport is also an unremitting critic of the law of effect. He accepts the validity of the law for animals, young children, and for the relatively mechanical and blind learning tasks of human adults. But the hedonistic law of effect is not accepted as normative for the complex systems of human learning. At best, it is a secondary law of learning.

Instead of learning as the result of tension reduction, there are times in the adult life when he learns as a result of tension. Allport uses the illustration of mispronouncing a word in public with the consequent ridicule and shame. Here there is tension. Here there is dissatisfaction, but he is certain that he will learn the correct pronunciation.

There is a determination to avoid such suffering in the future, but at the present there is no drive reduction. Again, he writes of having read and learned the essential content of *Mein Kampf* in 1940. He experienced increasing emotional tension, mounting discomfort, and acute dissatisfaction. He asks rhetorically, Where was the law of effect? "If the examples I have just given can be manipulated to fit the hedonistic formula, then I maintain that the formula is so loose as to be worthless. In no intelligent sense in any of these cases was a tension reduced, a discomfort relieved, or a satisfaction derived." [52]

Satisfaction may have a legitimate function in learning as an indicator for the person's perceptual processes, but it is not dynamically decisive. To say that one persists in a difficult and pain-experiencing task because of self-administered rewards is dangerous reasoning. "Would it not be truer to say that in persisting I am refusing to use the indicators of pain and pleasure, and am treating these two impostors just the same?" [53]

Guthrie's contiguous conditioning does not demand reward as an explanation of learning. Yet his experiments are as rigorous as any of those developed by reinforcement theorists. He thinks that reinforcement is inadequate because of a necessary ambiguity whenever the attempt is made to define the meaning of pain and pleasure.[54] Not only is the law of effect rejected because of ambiguity of definition but because the evidence does not permit its unqualified endorsement. He wonders how the law of effect can account for learning situations in which there is increase of tension. "Only for the senescent does drive reduction have a certain plausibility as a universal requirement of learning as a guide of life." [55]

The weakness of the law of effect as a fundamental postulate is further illustrated by the change of mind of a former confirmed reinforcement theorist.

In 1946, O. Hobart Mowrer stood firmly for the law of effect as a primary law of learning. Organisms learn only when a tension is reduced, a discomfort relieved, or satisfaction derived. Actual reinforcement may follow from either primary or secondary drive reduction. Conditioning was understood as a subsidiary form of learning.[56]

Later, Mowrer came to reject the one factor of reinforcement in favor of a two-factor theory involving conditioning and reinforcement. This stand was indicated in his work of 1950.[57]

At the Kentucky Symposium in 1954, Mowrer had modified his two-factor theory in a direction more related to human needs. Thorndike's law of effect was repudiated. Instead of rewards strengthening stimulus-response bonds and punishment weakening them, rewards and punishment produce secondary reinforcements, and secondary motivations develop through conditioning. Attitudes, meanings, and expectations are learned as secondary reinforcements.[58] Conditioning to significant stimuli is appropriate to a certain point, and then a more complex system must take over. This is understood as consciousness, a continuous-computing device or process. Instead of a machine model, learning should follow the model of the thermostat, an instrument of control. Mowrer concludes that there is a division of labor between learning as a purely unconscious, automatic process and conscious judging, deciding, and acting. It is only when learning is so conceived that it is applicable for understanding human behavior. In fact, Mowrer prefers to say that learning as a term should be limited " to the acquisition of inner meanings which are then evaluated and used to arrive at the particular [often novel] decision and action which the total situation seems most to warrant." [59]

A second weakness of reinforcement theory is its inadequacy to explain productive thinking. There may be knowledge acquisition in reinforcement, but there is no credible solution to the problem of understanding. Trial-and-error learning presumes a certain amount of helpless stupidity before a response can occur, be rewarded, and hence, be learned. After the reward is given, there may still be a certain amount of trial and error on the next occurrence of the stimuli. Learning has taken place, but it has been with the subject blindfolded!

Thorndike's theory is based on the assumption that bonds are constantly being strengthened or weakened according to consequences. Once there have been thousands of bond combinations, the organism is able to utilize the proper associations. If past connections were not present, it would never be possible to solve a new problem. But Thorndike never devotes himself to a study of highest thought other than to assume all problem-solving is a matter of manipulation or mental trial and error.[60] It may be indicative of his orientation that the word "understanding" does not appear in the index of his *The Psychology of Learning.* Hilgard concludes his survey of Thorndike's connectionism with this observation: "Thorndike's preoccupation with bonds has insured that we turn to others, not Thorndike's followers, for a more careful appraisal of the role of meaning and understanding."[61]

Hull's reinforcement theory is a no more reliable answer to the problem of higher mental processes in man. His theoretical system is sophisticated, but since he assumes a basic identity between lower and higher mammals, he has turned from human evidence and confined his study primarily to the rat. He has written: "It may be added that most of these postulates have been based on the behavior of lower organisms, particularly the rat, in the belief that the behavior of all mammals operates according to the same primary laws. Humans have the added capacity of speech, symbolic behavior, with its accompanying advantages to the higher mental processes. Whether this introduces any primary behavioral laws remains to be determined."[62] While he is open to other sources, he never sees fit to investigate whether there are any differences between higher and lower mammals. Confidence is shaken in a system that explains human learning without human evidence.

Miller and Dollard's system fares no better when an explanation of the higher mental processes is sought. The status of learning theory is hardly improved by listing reasoning as a function of cue-producing responses. True, language and other symbols are involved in reasoning. But the rational experience itself seems left to chance. In connection with their position, Maier asks, " What causes a person to ask himself *good* questions? Many other responses can be elicited by a situation. . . . Surely, a selective process must operate, and a selection of the right question by random trial and error would be a long process." [63] No necessary answer is forthcoming on the basis of reinforcement postulates.

It is concluded that too many lacunae exist in reinforcement theory for it to be judged inclusive as the one theory of human learning.

### *Conditioning Theory*

1. Strengths

Conditioning theory as espoused by Guthrie commends itself through its parsimonious character. There is no worry about reducing drives, relieving tensions, and achieving satisfactions. All learning is held to be the contiguous association of response and situation when the response is elicited. Limiting learning to the simple relationship as defined means that Guthrie's theory is easy to communicate. Whether the strength of simplicity may be a hidden handicap must await an evaluation to be offered in the " weaknesses " section.

The case for conditioning rests on substantial experimental evidence. Neutral stimuli are given active strength. From the facts at hand, it does not matter whether conditioning is explained in terms of contiguity between substitute stimulus and response as in Guthrie or in the temporal association of unconditioned and conditioned stimuli. In either case, a formerly neutral stimulus acquires the power to prompt responses. Virginia Voeks's study of eyelid conditioning indicates there is a high probability that no stimulus-response connection is gradually strengthened with repeated reinforcements as in Hull. Instead, it seems that Guthrie's position is supported. Every stimulus-response connection appears to be established suddenly in an all-or-none fashion.[64]

Conditioning further commends itself because conclusions from the laboratory have been corroborated by life experiences as well as psychotherapy.

The operation of conditioning often results in children acquiring unanticipated learning! They often appear disobedient because they become conditioned to disobedience. Guthrie cautions that by calling a child when he is occupied or when the parent is not serious about insisting on his coming, the child is conditioned to the mother's call as a sign that she really does not care. The call is a formerly neutral stimulus given meaning exactly opposite to that intended.[65]

Learning to read is a further confirmation of conditioning. Logically, there is no necessary connection between the " mark " on a page, the spoken word, and the meaning. Yet by speaking a word and pointing to the combination of letters, the neutral stimulus of mark-on-page now elicits the same idea or object designation as the spoken word. The written word has become the conditioned stimulus and the act of reading the conditioned response.

John McGeoch and Arthur Irion call attention to the fact that fears are often learned through conditioning " by the association of a previously neutral stimulus with an unconditioned stimulus of a painful nature."[66] Generally, persons are able to accept a variety of fears without disastrous results. Yet in combination with other factors, the conditioned reaction of fear may lead to the disintegration of personality. When this occurs, there is need for re-education. Harry Stack Sullivan notes that malevolence may develop in children because action which once resulted in tenderness now issues in rejection. The home situation is a sign that the world is against the juvenile. Through acts of love and acceptance, however, the home situation may again become a sign of personal security and well being.[67]

2. Weaknesses

The strength of simplicity in Guthrie's theory may also be a weakness. In view of the fluid character of learning theory, any theory may be considered suspect that attempts to crystallize itself into a set form. Some aspect of learning may be omitted without being brought to awareness because it has been concealed beneath simplicity of expression. Hilgard is uneasy about the finality that Guthrie's system appears to have. "Experimental controversies finally get resolved as we learn more about the independent variables that modify the measured consequences. No matter how these issues get resolved, Guthrie's system remains unchanged." [68]

Buswell wonders about the practical implications of following Guthrie's position of delaying a stimulus until the desired response is likely to occur. "Is the teacher then never to ask a question until he is confident it will be answered correctly? and by what occult power will he know when the time is ripe?" [69]

A more fundamental criticism of conditioning is its difficulty in dealing with the higher order of human processes. There is justification for conditioning's attempt to account for the numerous experiences of stereotypy in man, but it appears to overlook distinctive, mature human behavior. The choosing man may become lost in the confluence of stimuli and responses. Yet the choosing man does agree to conditioning or refuses conditioning under certain circumstances. The attempt at "re-education" of the American soldiers captured during the Korean War is illustrative of both points. Some men were conditioned, but many more would not permit stimuli to be effective at the center of their action processes. The subtle propaganda stimuli were foreign intruders to be cast out. They violated the self-structure deemed significant by the prisoners. If conditioning is an absolute law for all learning, why were not all the men conditioned according to the wishes of the Communist " teachers "? Something similar is involved in John Bennett's description of the persistence of autonomous thought among Soviet intellectuals. " Soviet education has not produced a generation possessed by the total Communist world view." [70] In spite of the presence of that view, the basic concern is for personal and human values. At the place where the self is in danger of being engulfed, it has the tenacious characteristic from time to time of asserting its functional autonomy.

Melville Herskovits accepts conditioning as a valid description of enculturation, the assimilation of the traditions of the group as guides to action. However, he does not think it is altogether satisfactory. Conditioning is useful for the early life of the person. Here he is " instrument rather than player." Another process must enter in at a later point where choice is operative. He calls this " reconditioning." Change " is the result of discussion, of consideration by individuals who must alter their individual modes of thought and action if it is accepted, or argue preference for established custom in rejecting it." [71] Mowrer considers conditioning adequate as a beginning, but then consciousness must take over. Here information is received, evaluated, and summarized as decisions, choices, and intentions.[72] For Allport, the popular principles of learning, including conditioning, may be good ones, but " when the ego is engaged they operate in a contingent fashion." [73] It is hoped that future theories of learning will not be so peripheral to the ego as one of the structures of the self.

Again, conditioning holds that all learning is under the control of situations, events, or persons. Guthrie asks, " What does the principle of conditioning mean in the form of practical advice? Largely this, that if we wish to have any act of our own or of another *under our control* so that we can elicit it on occasion, we must go through the following procedure." [74] To base learning on the control of another person presupposes that the " instructor " is fully capable of determining absolute rather than proximate goals for the " student." Therefore, stimuli can be selected that will issue in the kind of educated person desired irrespective of the learner's wishes.

Were the evidence for conditioning incontestable, then it would be necessary to come to terms with it. But the case for it is by no means certain. The emergence of original personalities negates the thesis that learning may be totally under the control of another. If conditioning were absolute, then conformity should be the result. This is not true as the history of culture, including political structures, indicates.

Whereas totalitarian societies thrive on their ability to control the changing experiences of persons, democratic communities deny that learning must be under the control of others. The logic of the democratic spirit finds the principle of control in conditioning abhorrent. In fact, if conditioning were the only law of learning, it is difficult to see how it would be possible for democracy to emerge and grow. This has been a concern of Allport. " Up to now the ' behavioral sciences,' including psychology, have not provided us with a picture of man capable of creating or living in a democracy. These sciences in large part have imitated the billiard ball model of physics, now of course outmoded. They have delivered into our hands a psychology of an ' empty organism,' pushed by drives and molded by environmental circumstance." [75]

Adherence to the stimulus-response mechanism at the heart of conditioning theory places the theorist in the position of explaining the kind of learning of least significance to the educator. Not animal learning but human learning is the goal of education. In so far as conditioning theory fails to get beyond the individual as an animal, it suffers from a weakness which cannot be changed unless the theory itself is changed. This is a serious structural problem.

*Gestalt Theory*

1. Strengths

Gestalt theory has maintained its appeal through its emphasis on wholes rather than parts. Implications drawn from this central principle have influenced many who have been dissatisfied with mechanistic interpretations of human behavior. It is a strength of gestalt theory that it finds wider support than in the field of learning itself.

In his *Client-centered Therapy,* Carl Rogers acknowledges his indebtedness to gestalt psychology " with its emphasis upon the wholeness and interrelatedness of the cluster of phenomena which we think of as the individual." [76] Allport classifies psychological schools into Lockean and Leibnitzian traditions that treat man's mind as passive and active, respectively. He clearly identifies himself with the Leibnitzian view of the active intellect and consequently with gestalt theory.[77]

In Koffka and to some extent in Köhler, gestalt theory has reintroduced the ego concept to psychology. This is a dynamic process co-extensive with the physical person but not identical with the individual. The martyr going to the stake may have experienced mutilation of the body, but his ego is unaffected. On the other hand, physical aspects of the individual may be a part of the ego: " my foot," or " my disfigured face." The ego is also more than thought. People have had dreams in which they were requested to answer questions. In the dream, they were unable to answer but " another " person in the dream could give the correct response. Obviously, the " two " persons were identical.[78]

The positing of an ego or an active tension system within the individual corresponds more closely with what persons observe in others and know in themselves. It is a dimension closed to the animal laboratory but one which is necessary for any theory which purports to explain human learning. Gestalt theory has suggested the theoretical framework in which ego functioning may find legitimate expression. This is a fundamental strength for a theory of human learning. Furthermore, the man which emerges in gestalt thought is no mechanical object. As interpreted by Combs and Snygg, man is a being affected by his environment but also one capable of shaping his destiny. Man is a responsible agent.[79]

Rogers' observation of persons undergoing therapy supports the thesis of an active intellect responding and refusing to respond to stimuli. Perceptions at variance with conceptions of the self are not admitted to awareness. Whether these perceptions are complimentary or derogatory, they are excluded as intruders. Far from being the passive recipient of stimuli, " the individual appears to be able to discriminate between threatening and nonthreatening stimuli, and to react accordingly." [80]

A second major strength of gestalt theory is its work on perception. This was one of its original interests. The question that has disturbed gestaltists is this: If stimulus-response psychology is correct, why are objects not always perceived in the same manner? The same stimuli are operative. Gestalt theory contends perception is a function of the organization of stimuli by perceiving organisms. The person's center of attention modifies what is perceived.

Support for the gestalt position on perception is given in an autobiographical report of a college student as related by Snygg. The boy in question had been an excellent student in the seventh grade, passing the regent's examination for eighth-grade arithmetic. During the summer, he had been discovered in an action which his mother said would turn him into an idiot. The next year's work was barely passed satisfactorily. Arithmetic was failed twice. After the school had administered an intelligence test, the boy learned from another student that his score of 90 was about average. At that point, the boy's grades improved. Later he read a book in which eminent authorities agreed that the threat of idiocy was without foundation. There followed a sudden jump in scholastic ability and he was graduated with fourth-place honors.[81]

Here was change not due to the accretion of one more fact. The boy's learning was limited and determined by *his* view of the situation. Another item of information resulted in a new personality pattern. The crucial problem was not the kind of number of stimuli but how the *learner* perceived the total field. In the boy's personality change, there is modification of behavior as the result of transformation rather than addition.[82] The individual always reacts to the total field as perceived. The perception is, for the individual, reality.[83] Nothing is said about the objective truth of this reality. It may be true or false. But the individual acts in accordance with the way he sees the situation.

The gestalt approach to the higher mental processes of thinking and understanding is a third strength. Gestaltists attempt to explain how higher organisms, primarily human, solve problems without running off a series of previously learned habits until the correct solution appears. J. Edward Dirks has expressed this principle clearly: " Understanding and comprehension develop . . . not when a realm of reality thrusts itself upon the mind but to the degree that the person who is learning gives his devoted concentration to portions of reality as wholes and those subportions of wholes which are particulars." [84]

In summation, thinking is essentially a continuous sequence of organization and reorganization of the perceived field by an active intellect. Instead of assuming that learning is something done to persons through stimuli impinging from the outside, gestalt theory conceives of learning as something which goes on in a dynamic field of tension including the person, the problem, and the relationship between them.[85]

2. Weaknesses

Because gestalt theory has an approach which permits man to remain as a perceiving, choosing, thinking, and responsible individual, there are no serious weaknesses in its formulations. There may be argument that gestalt theory is relatively inadequate for all the problems raised by theories such as reinforcement and conditioning. It is true that gestalt theory lacks the precise experimental details of behaviorism. Yet it is this appreciation for larger concerns which makes it particularly appropriate for the complex experience of human learning. Therefore, a lack of answers to some of the problems raised by other theories is less critical because some laboratory situations really do not measure the full potential of the subject since the choices open to it are so limited. It is of greater import that gestalt theory is able to predict basic human learning issuing in understanding of the current problem and a reorganization of the self-structure.

It appears that the most apparent weakness of gestalt theory is less in the theory and more in the theorists. It has not appealed to sufficient theorists to cause them to go through the exacting discipline of formalization. This is not strange since the prevailing spirit of American psychology is behavioristic and committed to the thesis that higher learning can be inferred from work with simpler organisms. Neither has gestalt theory stimulated thinkers to perpetuate it as a distinct theory in the sense of conditioning and reinforcement. Many psychologists [86] are influenced by gestalt principles, but there are no gestalt theorists today as in the generation which produced Wertheimer, Koffka, and Köhler. This is unfortuate. If some theorist were motivated by gestalt rather than stimulus-response principles, in order to go back over basic research, suggest new experimental procedures, the field of learning theory could not help but be enriched and given fresh direction.

*Sign-Gestalt Theory*

1. Strengths

Tolman's theory has maintained its general outline through the years, but it is less a finished product than reinforcement theory. In spite of the lack of precision, Tolman's insights have been a corrective to the dominant stimulus-response school in America. He has made it intellectually respectable to speak about cognitions as well as habits. Knowledge of means to goals is acquired. Active organisms are observing what patterns lead to others and finally to solutions.

Knowledge of meaningful relationships is gained with a minimum of extraneous trial-and-error effort. The organism " knows " what it is doing. However, as a behaviorist, he is less willing to specify an ego-structure or the enduring existence of the self as the efficient cause of distinctively human behavior. His use of terms such as " cognitive maps," " means-end-relations," " signs," and " expectations " are related to the gestalt emphasis upon reorganization and restructuring of the perceived field. Accordingly, meaningful behavior on the part of the learner is highlighted.

Tolman's stress of sign-gestalt formation as an alternative to learning only under reinforcement is an additional strength because it tends to widen an understanding of learning. There is more than a simple association of stimuli and responses under control. Reinforcement is viewed as important for performance but relatively neutral for learning. What happens is that reinforcement confirms or refutes the expectancy that the desired goal-object is where it was anticipated to be. Henceforth, the cognitive map of the situation is shown to be correct or incorrect. " The correct response becomes a sign for the sort of significate to be expected as a result of this correct response." [87] The organism then performs in virtue of the built-up sign relationship, plus the conditions of the moment. While the true nature of trial-and-error learning is the discovery of the proper sign-gestalts, learning involves more than separate units. Trial and error becomes a matter of field organization, with the environmental field always held together by the means-end stimuli.[88]

2. Weaknesses

Tolman set out to develop a cognitive learning theory within a behavioral framework. Communication with stimulus-response psychologists is made easier but perhaps at the price of presenting a theory of limited value for understanding human learning. His experimental work is primarily in the rat laboratory too. When he defines his theory of learning, as does Hull, he often slips into terminology specifically related to what a rat may be doing in a maze. He describes thought as " running-back-and-forth," or he speaks of " means-end-relations " which are terms growing out of animal studies. The translation of such terminology into human learning problems is often difficult. Not much assistance is offered in this regard.

The learning of " cognitive maps " is probably superior to stimulus-response connections as a descriptive term, but it defies analysis. It may be just as valid to say that associations are being developed between stimuli and responses. Osgood wonders if Tolman's behaviorism really is not a thinly disguised mentalism. " Explaining rat behavior in terms of immanent expectations is merely a sophisticated anthromorphism . . . *unless* expectations are identified in a manner independent of the overt behavior supposedly mediated." [89]

For all of the admitted advance in learning theory that his cognitive emphasis has offered, his behavioristic orientation provides handicaps for human learning. Man as active self is not a working presupposition. Instead, primary concern is given to laboratory experiments with infrahuman subjects. If man's self activity were stressed instead of such less dynamic terms as hypothesis, expectancy, and cognitive maps, there would be less validity in referring to sign-gestalt as the " dilute American cognitive theory." [90] As a result, insight into human learning must wait upon wider investigations.

How functionally adequate and theologically accurate each of these theories is for the concerns of Christian nurture will be the subject for evaluation in Chapter V. In the meantime, attention must be given to the theological perspectives informing this study.

Whenever behavioral sciences are interrogated in Christian education, there can be no appropriation of their insights without going through the careful investigation of their theological significance. Appropriation without evaluation may result in mutually incompatible positions. Laboratory learning theory developed with infrahuman subjects may not be universally valid and universally applicable. Rather, as the investigation of learning-theory resources just completed indicates, *there are different kinds of learning with theories relevant to the problems specified.*

Before rejecting or affirming the learning theories described here, responsible theory-building in Christian education requires the probing of theological resources for authentic insights on the nature of learning in Christian nurture.

CHAPTER IV

# Theological Foundations for Learning

ONE OF THE PARAMOUNT NEEDS of the church is for it to give greater attention to the problem of learning the concerns of Christian nurture. Therefore, questions of process must be addressed to theology. This does not mean that learning theory insights are to be dismissed. On the contrary, they are to be utilized as servants of theology for the special concerns of the church. But theology has its distinctive contribution for process in nurture. This has not been heard as an integral part of the church's theory of learning.

The second function of theology is to provide a frame of reference through which any proposed theory of learning in the church may be validated. James Smart's observation on the lack of theological emphases by religious educators points to the need of theology to validate learning theory as well. The Christian educator has erred in assuming that "his subject is educational rather than theological." [1]

To provide theological foundations for process in Christian nurture and for the validation of learning theory conclusions, summary expositions are offered of the four doctrines assumed to have relevance for Christian nurture: revelation, man, the church, and the Holy Spirit.[2] As these are articulated, implications may be drawn for their contribution to an understanding of that learning anticipated through the continuing relationship with persons and with God in Christian nurture.

## Revelation

Revelation is basic to the existence of the Christian faith. In the view of Edwin Lewis, Christianity may be said to stand or fall by the reality of its claim to be grounded in revelation. " In Jesus Christ, the very fact of him, the preparation for him, what he was, what he did, how he did it, together with all that comes to pass where this is taken for truth — in this, God stands self-disclosed. So runs the Christian claim." [3]

What the church has tried to say in human language about matters of divine import is confessed to be based on revelation. Whether the church is speaking about man, atonement, God, or even the church itself, revelation is the point of departure and the place of return. It is the source and norm of the church's proclamation and practice, including the complex experience of learning in Christian nurture. To this end, the procedural side of revelation will be accented more than the substantive.

1. *Revelation is God's act in disclosing himself.*

According to Albrecht Oepke,[4] the root meaning of the cognate words for " revelation " is that something which has been covered, veiled, or hidden is now uncovered, unveiled, or made manifest. When men in the Bible attempt to explain what has happened to them in their experience of the hidden God, they are certain that he has drawn aside the veil. God has disclosed himself.

While in the Old Testament, Yahweh reveals himself as the Lord of history, as the holy and merciful One, and as the Creator and Sustainer of the world, it is clear that revelation means more than reports about what God has done. " Revelation is not the communication of supernatural knowledge and not the excitation of feelings of awe. Knowledge can, indeed, grow into revelation and the revelation of God is necessarily accompanied by numinous sensations (Ex. 19:16; Isa. 6:5) , but this is not revelation.

Revelation is rather characteristically the act of God. It is the unveiling of his essential hiddenness, the offering of himself in fellowship." [5]

In the New Testament, there is a similar understanding, according to Oepke. Revelation is the gift of the holy, merciful God to mankind lost in sin and death. It is the self-offering of the Father of Jesus Christ. In Jesus Christ, God is continually removing the veil from himself.

To assert without apology that revelation is primarily God's act in Jesus Christ, however, does not limit revelation to the first three decades of the Christian era. Revelation as Jesus Christ is the culmination and the authentication of God's persistent movement toward man. Apart from Christ, we cannot know that God has really disclosed himself and is ever about to disclose himself to us in the present. But this is always his prerogative. Man cannot obtain insight into the will of God as a self-contained human achievement. John Baillie sees the problem of revelation as involving a distinction between the words " discover " and " disclose." " To disclose means to uncover, but in ordinary usage it does not mean to discover. I discover something for myself, but I disclose it to another." [6]

Revelation as God's sovereign act in Jesus Christ is a scandal to man who understands himself as the measure of all things. Designating knowledge of God as beyond the scope of human cognitive capacity appears to be moving against the tide of science with its impressive attainments. Nevertheless, whether it is popular to argue against the sufficiency of man or not, the essential dimension of revelation as God's act must be preserved or revelation is nothing.

For the Christian, revelation becomes both the resource and the means for realizing knowledge of God rather than speculations about him. Emil Brunner places revelation in its proper perspective: "It is a way of acquiring knowledge that is absolutely and essentially — and not only relatively — opposite to the usual human method of acquiring knowledge, by means of observation, research, and thought. Revelation means a supernatural kind of knowledge — given in a marvelous way — of something that man, of himself, could never know." [7]

Neither must revelation be equated with a mastery of Biblical information. This may be the means of revelation but cannot of itself guarantee it. When the most exacting skill has been attained in the exegesis and exposition of the Scriptures, revelation may not necessarily occur. Revelation is always the free decision of God even as Karl Barth has stated it: " Where the Word of God is heard and proclaimed, something happens which in spite of all interpretative skill cannot be brought about by interpretative skill." [8] Thayer's definition of revelation incorporates this same conviction: Revelation is " a disclosure of truth, *instruction,* concerning divine things before unknown . . . given to the soul by God himself . . . and so to be distinguished from other methods of instruction." [9]

God remains the initiator of his unveiling to man. This is not a point to be proved but a faith to be confessed. For the student of learning theory in the church, revelation as God's act of disclosure becomes one of the factors bearing upon the experience of faith learning. This is a dimension beyond the scope of the learning theories discussed above.

Revelation is God's self-manifestation. It is his persistent concern that persons be acquainted not *about* him but that they might know him. In revelation, there is an active Person involved in the process of nurture. If God is overlooked, comprehension of learning in the Christian faith must accordingly be truncated.

Learning the deepest concerns of the faith, therefore, is not wholly subject to human control. It is a gross oversimplification to assume that in all learning one must desire something, see something, do something, and receive something.[10] It is equally inadequate to speak of the deepest changes in persons as the result of a conditioned response because this depersonalizes man and turns God into a stimulus under the direction of the educator.

If revelation is God's initiative, whether revelation occurs is dependent upon him. It is the outthrust of the divine love, rather than the human desire which results in the most fundamental knowledge of God and of man himself. In revelation, man is grasped by God. Man does not receive revelation; revelation receives him. Johnson has drawn a valid implication from revelation as the divine initiative when he writes, "The primary factor in the educative relation . . . is something which is not manipulated or controlled by the educational process itself. It comes as a sheer gift of the grace of God. . . ." [11]

2. *Revelation is God's disclosure of himself to man.*

Now instead of concentrating upon the confession that God does reveal himself, the focus of attention is the object of revelation. To whom is the arm of the Lord revealed and who is to believe what is heard? The answer is that *man* is to hear God. What this entails for Christian nurture will be made clear shortly. Here it is affirmed that in God's speaking it is anticipated that there may be hearing. God is scarcely content to be calling down the empty rain barrels of the universe, as it were, in order to delight in the echo! He reveals himself to man and for the sake of man. This assumes that the character of man is such that the revelatory word does not return void but accomplishes its purpose. Barth has stated it this way: "To men are directed preaching and sacrament, to men the word of the prophets and apostles, to men the revelation of God himself in Jesus Christ, to men, therefore, the Word of God also. . . . If it is directed to them, it will obviously be known by them and therefore heard." [12]

But how is it possible for men to hear the Word of God? This question is the theological correlate to the problem of learning posed by Christian nurture. How may man come to such a knowledge and understanding of God that the deepest learning of the self may occur? The answer is that man must perceive revelation as God's disclosure. The receiving of revelation is as important as the giving.

Man perceives revelation through his rational faculties as developed through normal educative processes. Yet the acceptance of revelation as revelation is conditioned by man's finitude. God must guide the minds of those who interpret the events so that they may grasp their revelatory character. Baillie writes that "the illumination of the receiving mind is a necessary condition of the divine self-disclosure." [13]

Two implications for learning theory are involved in revelation as God's unveiling of himself to *man*.

In the first place, revelation for man requires an active human intellect. This is evident in the symbol of "word" which the Bible uses to communicate the idea of revelation. A word is meaningless unless there are active persons capable of hearing and expressing what is heard. The revelatory word, accordingly, suggests the highest regard for man as an intelligent learner. If the word of God is addressed to man, then man's intellectual processes are able to utilize what is received.

The active intellect is crucial at the point of response to revelation. Here God addresses the understanding in order to elicit a response. Such a response is not to be construed as of the same dimension as the stimulus-response theories of learning. In the latter, the stimulus comes from without and the response is expressed in behavioristic terms. Once the proper correlation of stimulus and response has been achieved, repetition of the stimulus, other things being equal, causes the same response. In revelation, there is the free, courageous response of an active self struggling to determine the character of the response which he will permit himself to make.

Again, revelation for *man* implies that he may affect its reception. Where there are active intellects, there may the distortion of revelation be possible. The distortion is an option because of the human situation in which revelation is heard. God wills to give himself to persons and awaken basic trust in himself. Where people have had their trust of others perverted, they may practice withdrawal to the point where they become effectively insulated from the power of God. Howe has indicated that " there are many lonely, anxious, and alienated people, who, though they may use the symbols and ceremonies of a religion of reconciliation, do not and cannot enter into a true relationship with God or man." [14] In the Biblical witness, human needs determine how revelation is received even though the content of revelation is always God. Moses expresses revelation within the framework of law, while John speaks of what he has heard as love.

In terms of learning theory, revelation means that while persons cannot guarantee or compel revelation, they may so structure the learning situation that the full force of it may be blunted or even thwarted. It implies further that persons may structure a situation in such a manner that the likelihood of revelation is increased. The channel for revelation is open. Persons may be vehicles for revelation as well as hindrances, according to Jesus' portrayal of the soils in which the seed is planted (Luke 8:4-15).

3. *Revelation occurs in dialogue between God and man.*

Dialogue as a term represents reciprocal address and response. It is not the meeting of a Subject-object but the encounter between Subject-subject, the divine Self in relationship with the human self. As George Hendry writes, " God speaks his word, addresses it to man's understanding, and seeks to elicit an understanding response." [15]

To define the revelatory process as Person to person, communication argues for the preservation of a dynamic quality in the transaction. Yet it is just this dynamic quality which is always under threat from attempts to crystallize revelation as something which has occurred and must now be accepted according to a particular form. The revelatory process then becomes primarily a cognitive experience. If the form of revelation is acceptable to the individual, revelation is assumed to have occurred. A vigorous dissent must be registered whenever revelation is so domesticated and consequently rendered harmless. God then becomes far removed from the desperate circumstances in which man lives and moves. In short, man has awareness of God's existence but no sure access to the Father through Jesus Christ the Lord.

Perhaps the importance of revelation as dialogue may be apprehended afresh by momentarily stepping outside the Christian tradition to that of Islam. Kenneth Cragg's analysis of the difference between revelation in the Scriptures and revelation in the Koran cites the offer of relationship in the Biblical witness as the distinguishing mark. Islamic revelation consists in words from God through the prophet Mohammed. The emphasis is upon the words themselves. In contrast, the Biblical revelation is essentially "a relationship to be received and experienced." [16] It is personal communication in which God imparts himself even as man responds in faith. The impartation is not a book but the Lord himself.

There must be no searching for revelatory reports in the Scriptures without the consciousness that here and now God is disclosing himself in terms of man's asking. This is not to say that God is helpless until man asks the right question. Rather, within the answering, man is given grace to make legitimate inquiries to which revelation provides answers. Paul Tillich has recalled us to the intensely personal nature of revelation. This is the moment "in which the divine Spirit grasps, shakes, and moves the human spirit." At the same time, revelation is received "only in the depth of a personal life, in its struggles, decisions, and self-surrender." [17]

Since revelation takes place in dialogue between God and man, the way is provided for depth learning. Man is confronted by a Person who offers himself in love and judgment.

The response of significance for learning through revelation is never automatic. Neither is a specific response assured. Dialogue can never be ordered but occurs in freedom even as Martin Buber has described it, " It is not that you *are* to answer but that you *are able*." [18] Revelation is just this open invitation to man to answer. It includes the possibility of saying, " No." It may be that even in the negative response there has been genuine encounter which on a future occasion may be changed to the affirmative because God has respected man's personhood. In the mutual address and response between God and man, man learns who he is, and who God is. Man's dimly perceived understandings become enlightened. Potential knowledge has become actual. Job expressed it in these words: " I had heard of thee by the hearing of the ear, but now my eyes see thee " (Job 42:5).

This apparently is what Paul Tournier means when he characterizes dialogue as resulting in faith and real knowledge of God. In terms of this study, Tournier is writing of learning through the disclosure of God to man. " Telling God frankly what I have to say to him and listening to what he has quite personally to say to me — this is the dialogue which makes me a person, a free and responsible being. . . . Even if it is only a fugitive moment, that moment is creative: the person awakes and emerges." [19]

4. *In revelation, the event and the revelatory situation belong together.*

This further dimension of revelation is necessary to guard against any careless assumption that persons should expect direct communication with God independently from what he has already spoken. What is revealed in personal dialogue must conform in all essentials with the historic revelation as witnessed by the prophets and the apostles. The New Testament is unaware of any new revelation unrelated to Jesus Christ.

Indeed, so intimately connected is the apprehension of

Christ with the event of God's personal disclosure through the Scriptures and the situation in which the witness is received, that the event and the revelatory situation belong together. " Neither the Ten Commandments nor the great commandment is revelatory if separated from the divine covenant with Israel or from the presence of the Kingdom of God in the Christ." [20] This means that revelation can only be received and communicated by those who participate in the revelatory situation. Only those for whom the matters under discussion are of ultimate concern can experience revelation.[21]

When inquiry is made of what this implies for learning in Christian nurture, the conclusion is that the church is the revelatory situation. Here is the community of the committed. Here is where communion with God is a matter of extreme urgency. Now knowledge of Biblical events is not presumed to be final knowledge; it is the foundation for participation in the Biblical events. Amos and Paul become cosharers with the present learners for God's nurturing of his people rather than as objects to be analyzed.

Charles Stinnette affirms participative action within a committed community as the model for the communication of Christian truth. " The genius of event is that it draws the spectator into participation. He who reads the Bible or gives his attention to Christian worship or offers a cup of water to the afflicted, as if to Christ, is apt to find himself caught up as a participant in the drama of salvation beyond his expectations." [22]

If the process and the revelatory situation belong together, then a knowledge of the Biblical witness to revelation within the context of a community of faith forms a unified factor for learning in Christian nurture and must be maintained as such.

## MAN

In 1953, J. Donald Butler presented a paper to the Golden Anniversary Convention of the Religious Education Association on " The Christian View of Man and the Meaning of Freedom and Authority in Education." [23] He contended that before a philosophy of education can be reconstructed in terms of religious values, attention must be given to several subjects. One of these areas is stated as follows: " Careful thought must also be given to the distinctive emphases in our Hebrew-Christian tradition which are normative in determining what a philosophy of education must be if it is to be in harmony with this tradition. . . . An example is the nature of man." [24]

If a normative view of man must be predicated for a responsible philosophy of education, it is also essential for any theory of learning in Christian nurture. To develop such a norm and to see some of the consequent implications of an understanding of man for learning is the immediate task.

1. *Man learns his identity in relationship.*

Every discipline seeking to comprehend the nature of man begins its inquiry with certain methodological assumptions, specified or otherwise. For example, it has been seen that behavioristic psychology attempts to maintain objectivity in its analysis through the use of animal rather than human subjects. The knowledge of human behavior is the result of a projection of knowledge about animals. It should be apparent that the validity of this approach is not scientifically demonstrable. It is based on the assumption that humans are substantially like animals.

In a like manner, Christian theology has a basic methodological assumption. It confesses that man cannot be fully defined apart from the revelation of God. Brunner's description of what this entails is both necessary and accurate. " The fact that man is what he is is not a merely human but a ' theological ' concern; he is not to be understood in himself, nor from that reason which is in him. He can be understood only in the light of that which stands ' over against ' him, the Word of his Creator." [25]

This does not mean that the biological, psychological, and sociological investigations are without integrity. They have a legitimate function to perform which cannot be filled by theology alone. After all, theology is not the foundation for discovering that with other creatures man shares a similar body which experiences states of strength and weakness, and ultimately death. Neither is theology necessary to specify the clusters of man's physical needs.

But theology is under obligation to inform man of the meaning of his creaturely relationships. It is one thing to observe a similarity in anatomical structure and function and another to define what difference this makes for being *man*. From the perspective of the Word of God, man resembles other creatures primarily because with them he has been created. This accounts for his dependence. He is not an autonomous being who has wrested control from his less-developed fellow creatures because of his superior brain and an opposable thumb. These may permit man to maintain his status. However, man fails to know his identity if he prides himself on his mastery of nature. Were this the case there would be no ground for restraints on his actions other than social pressure. Man would be beyond judgment. The theological factor sees man's superior creaturely status as a gracious gift of God, a command to exercise responsible dominion.

Furthermore, through God's Word, man affirms he is body, mind, and spirit, having the gift of life from the Father. Therefore, man is described as an individual self with self-integrity even though he is always dependent upon God for the consummate meaning of selfhood. Through consciousness, man has the capacity for surveying the world from a governing center. He is aware that he in some sense determines the course of action. He does not simply react; he acts.

Finally, there is a delimitation between man and other creatures which goes beyond that of either the category of the simple or complex organization of behavior. As a creature, man is a special concern of God. Only to man does the Word ascribe the image of God. Theologians are not agreed as to the precise meaning of the image of God, and no attempt needs to be made here to deal with the large body of literature on the subject. It is sufficient to be reminded that whatever the image of God is, it is intended to distinguish man from other creatures. Outwardly, man may not be so different, but in terms of the image in him, he is set apart in a unique manner. At a minimum, to be in the image of God suggests that man is on earth as God's representative. It is to perceive one's identity in relationship — with nature, yes, but also with other persons and with God.

Knowing oneself in relationship with other persons describes man as a social animal. Shortly after birth, the infant discovers there are other persons in the world whose wills may oppose his. Limits are set to his freedom. In the process, there comes the awareness dimly perceived but not verbalized that other persons are necessary for his own self-enhancement. As life becomes more complex, the interrelatedness of man and other persons takes on deepened meaning for the emergence of mature personhood.

At the same time, it is necessary to affirm that man's identity in relationships is a theological insight. It is his divinely determined destiny. God has said, " Let us make man in our image." Later, the narrator of the Genesis account reports that the creation was accomplished, and then the following words are added: " Male and female he created them " (Gen. 1:26-27) . This is a confession that an individual, according to the economy of God, cannot know himself alone. The husband is not independent, nor is the wife, but both are dependent upon the other. As is often asserted now, man becomes an I through the other, the Thou.[26]

Edmond Jacob observes that the normal word for man in Hebrew includes the double relationship of being related to nature and to other persons. " *Adam* is he who is taken from *adamah,* the ground — a weak, ephemeral being — and this name is also regarded as the proper name of the first man . . . yet, on the other hand, the sociological setting of man is expressed by the term *bēn adam,* ' son of man ' or ' humanity,' where *adam* denotes the collective type." [27] In his Word, God calls man out of individuality into community. Through the covenant community of Israel in the Old Testament and the church in the New Testament, personhood is learned in the tension between freedom and authority as embodied in the individual and the group.

Objective analysis of man in community has a place, but man's nature goes beyond analysis. To know the basic meaning of himself, man must begin with the faith, according to Reinhold Niebuhr, " that he is understood from beyond himself, that he is known and loved of God and must find himself in terms of obedience and the divine will." [28] Calvin thinks it significant for man's perception of himself that unlike the remainder of creation, man was not created by command. He was called into being through divine consultation and gradual transformation. Only man was created to live in communication with God's Word.[29] This gives man a divinely conferred position. Unlike the other animals, man is exalted. He may be in converse with his creator. In the continuing dialogue of word and worship, man learns that in God he lives and moves and has his being.

In brief, man learns his identity through the threefold relationship of nature, persons, and God. It is up to him to decide at what level he will be content to know himself. The immediate implication for Christian nurture must be that the nature of the relationship determines the depth of learning.

In relationship with *nature,* man discovers that he also participates in creaturely existence. This is the valid experience on which stimulus-response theories of learning are established. Man is an animal, and therefore conclusions reached about the way animals learn are appropriate for man as well in so far as there is a correspondence between man and the lower organisms. But theologically, there must be a question whether the depths of human learning have been plumbed where man's learning relationships are confined to the infrahuman level.

Man learns more of himself in relationship with other *persons*. Verbal and nonverbal forms of communication are available. Man learns the acts and the expressed feelings of another. Stinnette writes: " Man discovers himself *only* in relation to another. . . . [To] become himself, man requires the resistance of others as well as their acceptance, judgment as well as grace." [30] Since man learns in relationship, how man perceives these relationships determines how much of himself becomes understood. If persons are treated as objects, learning the more fundamental concerns of the Christian faith is severely handicapped. Where persons, however, find themselves in a community that communicates itself as nonthreatening, supportive, and redemptive, there man may find himself as a person once again. He is on the threshold of deeper learning about himself. Man is open to man in true communication.

Man's relationship with persons is the basis of psychotherapy and group process. Learning occurs within the therapeutic situation. It takes place between man and man. The quality of learning thus attained rises above that accessible to human and nature relationships. Yet the greatest learning eludes the interhuman community.

If man is created in the image of God, if man is intended for community, then man's highest learning can become a reality only in relationship with *God*. Man is most adequately known when he beholds himself as standing over against God, offering his creatureliness and capacity for transcendence. Man in his need receives divine answers. Where the human self is open to the divine Self, there is genuine learning. Johnson describes this as " faith relationship in which changes occur at the deepest level of the self-structure, resulting in a radical transformation of a re-creative and redemptive nature." [31]

2. *Man is called to be a covenant partner of God.*

As Mehl-Koehnlein defines him from the Biblical perspective, man " is, by God's act, a responsible being in God's sight." [32] This is evident in the responsibility implicit in the election of Abraham and the covenant mediated by Moses to Israel at Sinai. Apart from responsible existence, the prophetic call for Israel to fulfill its mission and the apostolic plea to repent and believe the gospel are without meaning. Man is the one who is responsible. Even when he acts irresponsibly, he always stands under the judgment of God. This places him in a radically different relationship with God than that which prevails for the other creatures.

Walter Eichrodt schematizes the Old Testament teaching of man as the one who is unconditionally responsible. " It may be affirmed without exaggeration that in no other people of the ancient East is the sense of responsibility of each member of the people so living, and the personal attitude so dominant." [33] Israel was aware that the basis of each person's responsibility was the fact that God had entered into a covenant relationship with it. Therefore, man may be understood Biblically as being a called covenant partner of God.

For Eichrodt too, man as a responsible person is implied in the prophetic call to repentance and faith. " This asks of the individual a conscious decision against the constraint of the collective will and against the pressure of a cultural development encouraged by the whole external situation." [34] Furthermore, man is never permitted the privilege of having confidence in an ideal image of personality at rest in itself. God is continually confronting man as a real " Other." It is in this confrontation " that man is able to affirm that personal value which God desires to give to him, thus realizing the destiny which gives his life both a context and a goal." [35]

Since man is called to be a covenant partner of God, this must mean his responsible existence touches on the possibility of learning as well as the way of learning.

In terms of the kind of man suggested by the most widely accepted theories of learning, this implication is singularly significant. It knows nothing of a man who is persistently reactive, who is ever enmeshed in his own responses. To become a covenant partner of God, man must have the power to choose to which stimuli he will respond, and what will be the nature of the response. As a responsible learner, man may treat clusters of stimuli as irrelevant. He may also select the one stimulus that may radically change his life. To accept one's nature as responsible being and to enter into personal decision-making is the essence of being a person.[36]

To be a covenant partner of God means to be held accountable for one's acts. Buber's insight on responsibility is illuminating. "Responsibility presupposes one who addresses me primarily, that is, from a realm independent of myself, and to whom I am answerable. He addresses me about something that he has entrusted to me and that I am bound to take care of loyally. He addresses me from his trust and I respond in my loyalty or refuse to respond in my disloyalty. . . ." [37]

Because the One to whom man is responsible is God, the meaning of responsibility is intensified. Were man viewed only at the organic level, he could not be held accountable for his organization of learning. His learned drives or his learned motives occur because of the correlation of stimuli and responses. But because man is a called covenant partner of God, automatic behavior is discounted. "I call heaven and earth to witness against you this day, that I have set before you life and death . . . ; therefore choose life." (Deut. 30:19.)

Since man is called to be God's covenant partner, God

obligates himself to man. This divine responsibility becomes a source for learning human responsibility. As a covenant partner, man is not alone in bearing the burden of decision-making. The divine Self who is free comes to man in his freedom as sustaining and supporting power.

3. *Man is a sinner.*

The Bible does not philosophize about the origin of evil. It confesses that man is a sinner. He is continually missing the mark. He is created for responsibility, but he departs from the divine purpose of creation. Man is to live in relationship with God and other persons, but at every turn the self asserts its independence and there is estrangement instead of harmony.

To say that man sins at every turn is by no means to deny the possibility of works of virtue and goodness. Man does rise to heights of self-sacrifice. What is intended by the doctrine of the universal involvement of man in sin is that *all* of his relationships are affected by the decision to live without the sense of responsibility to God. Avoiding God, man hides himself from his associates. Suzanne de Dietrich finds that Adam and Eve's concealment of themselves in the garden after eating the forbidden fruit is a powerful description of human beings in their sin. " They cannot even bear the thought of letting people see their true selves, for they are ashamed to disclose the nakedness of what they really are in body, heart, and mind. This is why humanity goes on living a lie, and why men hide not only from one another but from themselves as well." [38] Therefore, sin is hardly an abstract concept. It is the breaking of relationships between man and man and between man and God. One always sins against someone. Barriers to communication are erected where none are needed or desired. As a consequence, " the lonely crowd " is more than a figure of speech. It is a terrible reality where men live their lives on the edge of desperation. They want communion but by predetermining the conditions of the alliance. Here man supplants the rightful God through rebelling against him. Such is the pervasiveness of sin in human life.

However, the total involvement of man in the manifestations of sin in no way indicates that man is less free. As a responsible being, man does not sin out of fateful necessity but sins within his freedom.[39] In this freedom, man remains a creature accountable to God and beloved by him with possibilities for redemption.

For the learning theorist in Christian nurture, the reality of sin must be dealt with as a factor which may hinder or distort man's ability to learn the concerns of the Christian faith.

The concept of man as sinner means that his powers of apprehension and comprehension are impaired especially where the things of God are involved. Physical observation and technical prowess are not hindered apparently by man's sin. But sin is a hindrance to learning when man seeks to know the meaning of himself in the world and the meaning of other persons. This factor is as effective in limiting learning as is a deficiency in intellectual ability.

Man finds it impossible to restructure his field of relationships to fulfill their proper purpose. He notes that he gets in the way. His perception is distorted. Reality is what he perceives, but no frame of reference is acknowledged that may reveal that the present reality is unworthy of attention. Instead of causing man to love persons, sin causes him to become more proficient at using persons and loving things.[40] The divine initiative receives the responses of unbelief, self-love, and disobedience.

The presence of sin in man cautions theorists against giving in to a shallow optimism in a theory of learning for Christian nurture. Where optimum conditions of learning are present, for example, in the person's intelligence, motivation, and the competence of a teacher, there is no certainty that the concerns of the Christian faith will be learned. Because sin cannot be given a quantitative value for learning purposes does not militate against its consideration in a responsible theory of learning. Laboratory work in the development and testing of learning theory postulates would be impossible without the hypothesizing of certain "intervening variables" within the learning process. An intervening variable is an inferred relationship between the independent variable (stimulus) and the dependent variable (response). For some learning theorists, this is drive and for others it may be expectations. In either case, the intervening variable is not subject to proof. Its existence is considered necessary to give credence to the theory. For Christian nurture, then, sin is the factor which intervenes between the call of God and the overt human response.

4. *Man's destiny is to be re-created by Jesus Christ for eternal communion with God.*

The final word is not spoken when man is described as a sinner. Man is intended for life rather than death. This is the foundation for God's seeking love in the Biblical witness. As Eichrodt describes the Old Testament man, he is seen as "pressed to the limit of his earthly existence by the divine demand, and directed toward a new order whose only assurance lies in the promise of God." [41]

Apart from the promised realization of his true destiny in God, man is a creature with only utilitarian value. He is useful for what he can produce. If he fails, there is always another to take his place. Gilbert and Sullivan probably speak more prophetically than they intended when they have Ko-Ko in *The Mikado* sing, "Ive got a little list." After going through a series of human types who never would be missed were they executed by the Lord High Executioner, he closes by singing, "But it really doesn't matter whom you put upon the list, for they'd none of 'em be missed — they'd none of 'em be missed!" This is an all-too-true description of man in the midst of his vocations and social involvements. He lives, labors, and dies. Others come and society continues.

But in the plan of God, the expendable man becomes nonexpendable. He is given value beyond human norms. This is abundantly clear in terms of God's plan of salvation as unfolded through the centuries of time. Humanly speaking, it would have been so much better to have sent Christ as early as the time of Abraham to defeat the powers of sin, death, and the devil. Untold misery could have been avoided. Yet God for his own inscrutable purposes chose to work patiently, drawing man to himself with cords of love. Finally, in the fullness of time, God sent his Son for the redemption of man. Through faith in Christ, man appropriates to himself the meaning of his nature and destiny. Even though as Niebuhr writes, " sin is overcome in principle but not in fact," [42] the issue is decided. Man realizes his true destiny is to be re-created by Jesus Christ for eternal communion with God. This is the case because Christ is himself the true man. He is " the origin and the goal of the humanity created by God and destined by him for communion with him and with one another." [43]

The learning-theory implication drawn from man's destiny in Christ is the primary basis for optimism in learning the concerns of the Christian faith. Since man is intended for Jesus Christ, God is involved in any action that leads man to accept his destiny. Whether the concerns of Christian nurture become learned must be God's decision. This is not a ground for general passivity on the part of man. It is the only basis on which man may be considered competent to guide another to the place where learning may occur.

## THE CHURCH

An understanding of the church enters into a discussion of learning theory in Christian nurture because of the function of community in learning. Community is defined by Sherrill as " *a body of relationships which affect the becoming of its individual members.* A community ' does something to ' the people who compose it, and they in turn do something to it, as the people of the community interact with one another."[44]

If the church as a community is only one more sociological entity which affects persons, then it offers no more profound insights for learning than any other community. However, if the church is viewed as within history and yet above history, as a fellowship of sinful people and yet a called community of God, this should have wider implications for the learning process. It may be stated provisionally that how the church communicates is less a matter of speech and more a matter of being.

Continuing the procedure found useful for " revelation " and for " man," the church will be defined through summary statements and more direct implications for learning theory drawn from them.

1. *The church is the covenant community of God.*

Originally, the Greek word *ekklēsia,* translated as " church " in the New Testament, was a secular rather than a religious term. Karl Schmidt notes that from the time of Thucydides, Plato, and Xenophon, *ekklēsia* is the gathering of the people of Athens and other Greek cities. " The derivation is simple and significant: the assembled citizens are the *ekklētoi* (called out) , i.e., those who have been summoned by the herald."[45] *Ekklēsia* comes into Christian thought by way of the Septuagint, where it is the usual rendering of the Hebrew *qahal,* a congregation or assembly. Now the fundamental issue of *ekklēsia* is less in the fact of a gathering and more in the identity of the one doing the calling. As Bishop Newbigin has written, " It derives its character not from its membership but from its Head, not from those who join it but from Him who calls it into being."[46]

Instead of a herald announcing tidings of something with which he may be only vaguely familiar, Christians acknowledge that they are gathered by God for important business. They are called out of their comfortable individualism to a corporate witness that Jesus Christ is Lord. To be sure, in the history of Christian experience some have interpreted the calling out as requiring a withdrawal from the sinful world. However, *ekklēsia* at its best is much more positive in its implications. It is an assembly that seeks to obey God within the world.[47] The theme of the World Presbyterian Alliance meeting in São Paulo, Brazil, in 1959 was "The Servant Lord and His Servant People." Here the church becomes a community that recognizes it is covenanted to Jesus Christ in obedience not for the sake of an organized social structure but for the glory of God and the service of man.

According to F. W. Dillistone, convenantal society views itself as purposive rather than as a natural social group. It does not dwell upon a structure already in existence. It conceives of the development of a new social order based upon the willingness of two partners to come to a purposive relationship through bridging a chasm that has formerly prevailed. No easy process of establishing the relationship is presumed. "The actual coming together constitutes a critical occasion of unusual solemnity and is normally marked by symbolic words and actions designed to bear witness to the irrevocable character of the new relationship thereby established." [48]

Viewed from this perspective, the Old Testament is a history of a people's struggle to fulfill the implicit meaning of being God's covenant community. The people do not choose God, but God chooses Israel (Deut. 7:7-9). Although there was probably never more than a minority who felt intimately identified with God in solemn covenant, these become the salvation of Israel. The remnant as expressed through the prophets ever called Israel to its true vocation as a community committed to be a royal priesthood to the nations. Later, God speaks of abandoning the old covenant in the interest of a new relationship to be consummated (Jer. 31:31-33).

The New Testament portrays Jesus Christ as the one who initiates this new covenant community not only through the calling of men to be his disciples but also in the covenant meal shared with them on the night he was betrayed. Here Jesus proclaims an identity of relationship with the Old Testament idea of the covenant community. He stands in the tradition of " the law, the prophets, and the writings." Discussing the implications of the Last Supper for its significance to the covenant community, Jesus is seen by Dillistone as investing his disciples with authority and partnership in his royal purpose. " In that hour the covenant community took shape and the Old Testament promise of the new covenant began to be fulfilled. Henceforth there existed in the world a community that had been taken into covenant relationship with God through Christ and which was committed to the task of calling men of all nations to enter into the same relationship and to become heirs with them of the promised Kingdom of God." [49]

Unless the church maintains its identity as such a community, a central emphasis is neglected to the impoverishment of the Biblical meaning of the church. Traditionally, the Reformed family of churches has tended to preserve this sense of communal responsibility. Men do not enter the church as a natural right but as a result of the divine initiative and the response of faith. In word and sacraments, the church proclaims its election and its acceptance of the covenant of grace. Although this is a dynamic view of the church, it has an obvious defect were this the only position. Bishop Newbigin has criticized the view of the church as existing where the word and sacraments are rightly preached and administered: " It gives no real place to the continuing life of the church as one fellowship binding the generations together in Christ. It makes of the church practically a series of totally disconnected events in which, at each moment and place at which the word and sacraments of the gospel are set forth, the church is there and then called into being by God's creative power." [50]

When the question is asked how the church as a covenant community presents implications for learning theory in its nurture, the answer must be related to the fact of purpose. This is at the heart of the covenant concept.

In Jesus Christ, God forms persons into a special community. This is always God's decision rather than man's desire for association. Therefore, the purpose of the church is for more than personal enrichment; it is to bear witness in the world according to what God has done in the covenant community and is about to do for those beyond it. This is both proclamation and nurture.

Tournier declares that science knows nothing of purpose; it knows only causality.[51] In spite of this fact, the church has often been a nearsighted Sir Launfal in quest of the Holy Grail in the far country of behavioral sciences while neglecting its own distinctive insights for process. Nurture through a purposeful community may be the Grail at home.

There is learning in the very decision of commitment to be within the community. Stinnette stresses that "first and foremost the means of communication in covenant community is derived from the fact that one has committed himself to an ongoing life which is characterized by the abiding presence of the Lord and Redeemer of history." [52]

Within the community there is heard how God has acted in behalf of his people. The past is now not an item of museum interest. It is a necessary part of the present. To be sure, churches may rehearse the history of God's people objectively, and the learning of this history may occur according to theories adequate for any kind of knowledge. However, if the nature of the church as a partnership with God is taken seriously, then the learner stands within a learning situation that goes beyond the apprehension of facts. The covenant history is now the learner's history. The covenant concerns are his concerns. Not only have the Israelites been called to decision concerning God, but the learner in the present is also challenged to make an inherited faith his own. There is learning in this dynamic community which anticipates that something of ultimate significance is ever about to happen in the learner's life. Not only is this true in the actual exposition of the Word, it is also relevant where the community shares in the sacraments. If these are viewed as God's acts and man's response in dramatizing the origin and purpose of his people, there is a learning potential which can effect changes in the self. Where God's people come together, there is more than group warmth. There is power for learning the concerns of Christian nurture which is not available elsewhere.

This is what Grimes apparently has in mind when he writes that it is possible to teach religion in the public schools, and in other groups, "but only as the quality of life of any group reaches a consciously Christian level does Christian nurture occur." [53] His position is also probably given empirical support in the English school situation as reported by Basil Yeaxlee. The English Education Act of 1944 requires religious instruction and daily corporate worship in all schools supported by public funds. Parents have the option to withdraw their children from these experiences on grounds of conscience, if they wish. Now after seventeen years of operation, the experiment is found deserving of support but the results have not fulfilled expectations for education into Christian living. Yeaxlee concludes: "Taking all the Christian forces and activities into account, however, the progress that has been made and the developments that may be hoped for, we are confronted by the stark fact that thousands of school leavers appear to be little if any better for all the efforts that their teachers have made to impart at least a knowledge of the most important Biblical facts and truths, the elements of Christian belief, and the principles of Christian conduct." [54]

Yeaxlee wonders if one of the causes for falling short of the objective is a communication problem. Teachers and students are not speaking the same language of faith. Their presuppositions and experiences in life must be taken into consideration more than has been done. It seems to me that to speak of communication involves more than identification of the value structure in which two groups may operate. It is not less than this, however. A lack of substantial improvement in the religious life of the English students is related, rather, to the problem of nurture within a purposeful community. More is required for nurture than at least two persons talking about matters religious. The concerns of Christian nurture can only be communicated within a committed community.

2. *The church is the body of Christ.*

If the weakness of the covenant community is its lack of correspondence with the whole people of God throughout time, the strength of the church as the body of Christ is its continuing identity. It does not depend for its validity upon each successive affirmation of faith by its members. The church persists as a structural totality ordained by God. To be a Christian is to be in the church. One cannot profess Jesus Christ as Lord and yet be out of communion with others who have also been fashioned as God's people. The church as the body of Christ is nothing less than the culmination of a relationship that began with the calling of Abraham, Isaac, and Jacob and continues into the present. God does not first initiate an idea, but he forms a people.[55] This indicates that the church is revealed as having a form and a life. In brief, the church is an organism and the essence of organism according to Dillistone is that of " a central source of life pouring vitality through every part of an ordered structure. . . ." [56]

Dillistone goes on to describe the organic view of society as stressing the common origin of its members and as a consequence the corporate character of society's life. The collective whole has life and is capable of behavior similar to that of the individual unit. For this reason, the word " body " has had wide appeal in describing the organic view of society in general and the church in particular.[57]

The organic view of society as given in the Old Testament is intensely personal. The body functions harmoniously, but the personality of the tribal leader becomes the personality of the group. Israel might have priests, but the whole nation acts as a priesthood. As the nation grew numerically a parallel idea developed. A group within Israel or even an individual can express corporate personality. This is shown, for example, in the " remnant " and the " servant " passages.[58]

A similar motif is present in the New Testament. If the Messianic terms " Son of Man " and " Servant " are understood as expressions of corporate personality, they can be described as the body of the Messiah, the body of the Servant or the body of the Son of Man. The Johannine account is more specifically organic. There is the allegory of the vine and the branches in which the branches are dependent upon the parent stock for life. The intimate union implicit between the Good Shepherd and the flock is also organic. As another attempt to comprehend the close relationship between Christ and people, the temple is described as the Lord's body. If it is destroyed, he will reconstitute it with larger significance.[59]

The Pauline letters are especially rich in affirming the church as the body of Christ. During the interim between the ascension and the Parousia, the church lives the Messiah's life on earth. " In their union with him, the members find their true union with one another: in the pattern of the Messiah's earthly life, the church finds the true pattern of her own." [60] The Ephesian and Colossian letters indicate a shift of emphasis. " Fullness " is there related to both Christ and the church. If the fullness of the Godhead dwells bodily in Christ, he in turn gives this fullness to the church. There is participation in his suffering and death but also in his glory.[61]

To be the body of Christ is to share in his life, death, and resurrection through the one loaf and the one cup. It is not to make the sacrament a mere memorial. It is a visible expression that Christ is ever head of the body. He presides at his Table, where his body is broken for the many. In the brokenness, the members find the source of their life and the direction for their mission. Having experienced redemption in Jesus Christ, members minister redemptively to one another and seek to bring others into this redemptive community. Here the sinner finds forgiveness, the broken receives healing, the weak is given strength and the fearful gains courage.

The resources of the universal redemptive community through the ages come to a focus in a particular community if the community sees itself as organically related to the church of the apostles. " Catholic " tradition interprets this according to a theory of succession of bishops. So firmly is this position held that it is the one fundamental issue which must be maintained if " catholic " groups are to consider union with the " noncatholic " bodies. Yet apostolicity is not necessarily a matter of tracing an episcopal pedigree. It is doing the work of the apostles. It is engaging the forces of evil in their lair. It is persistently battering down the gates of hell in ways reminiscent of the apostles and their Lord in his incarnate life. Where a particular structure is absolutized, it is possible to forget that even structure is under the judgment of Christ. Indeed, nothing affirmed about the church as the body of Christ must be allowed to deny the possibility of sin in the church's life. Just as individuals redeemed by Christ sin, so is the church enmeshed in pride, disobedience, and lovelessness. Yet it is just this body in which Christ abides, forgiving and renewing it.

Since body is more than a metaphor, there must be implications for the total life of the church. In this distinctive fellowship, Christ's redemptive ministry finds expression not figuratively but actually. If a particular church does not redeem as well as mediate redemption, it is losing its claim to be the church.

Lest this appear to mean that the church is a savior alongside of the One who was crucified outside of Jerusalem, it must be made clear that the church is the body of *Christ*. What it is follows from who he is. Here persons perceive that God so loved the world that he became man in Jesus Christ. In their acceptance of God's acceptance of them, they know the reality of redemption. At the same time, the objective redemption wrought by Christ is confirmed by the redemption evident in the church. God is a participant in this community. As Sherrill writes, now " the processes of interaction are capable of carrying a corrective, redemptive, and re-creative power, which comes in from beyond purely natural processes, not violating those processes nor setting them aside, but able to transform them." [62] From this understanding, it must be concluded that Christian nurture is not separated from redemption. Redemption — if it is redemption — transforms the human self and nurture — if it is nurture — explores the ramifications of redemption. To the extent that this redemptive-nurture is real, there is also change in the self. Learning in spiritual depth is a possibility where nurture is identified with Christ's body. Here its members may be re-created as they participate in the life of the Lord.

Even as learning occurs within the redemptive community, there is also learning within the context of need and of the insufficiency of meeting this need. Persons learn that although the church is the body of Christ, it may sin. Therefore, there can be no absolute confidence that just because one is being nurtured in a community identified as the body of Christ, only grace will be communicated. Sin may also be learned! This is the shame of the church. But sin does not ultimately triumph. Because the church is his body, Christ is present in the midst of human estrangement. After the learner has identified himself with Christ's will, the way is opened for him to have his value orientation changed. In the reorganization of the self, one more area of life is surrendered to the Lordship of Christ. Such nurture within the body takes cognizance of the pervasiveness of sin and the adequacy of God's grace.

3. *The church is the community of the Holy Spirit.*

Identifying the church as the community of the Holy Spirit has integrity in itself and also provides us with a point of transition to the fuller treatment of the Holy Spirit in the next section of this chapter.

Although the church is most assuredly a covenanted, committed fellowship, a redemptive organism with historical roots, it is also a manifestation of God's life in the midst of a particular people. Menoud's assessment of the relationship between church and Spirit is incontestable. "The Spirit apart from the church would be energy without any instrument through which it could operate. The church without the Spirit would be a body without a principle of life."[63] Samuel Shoemaker thinks along similar lines. He takes issue with those who proclaim the church as the extension of the incarnation. Instead, he says that his conviction is growing that the real extension of the incarnation is the Holy Spirit. This must not mean a separation from the church, however. "But the church dare not claim to be the extension of the incarnation except as she is infused and indwelt by the Holy Spirit. Without this, the body is dead; and no dead body, however once alive, can be an extension of the life of Christ in the world."[64]

If the church is without life unless the Holy Spirit is present, this is not to say that the Spirit appeared on the scene only after Pentecost. The prophets were very conscious that whatever truth they spoke or whatever power motivated them, the Spirit of God was present. J. Robert Nelson criticizes attempts to deny the work of the Spirit in pre-Christian history as being so narrow as to be blasphemous.[65] At Pentecost, the same Spirit is encountered as known by the prophets, but the experiences of those led by the Spirit in relation to Christ are also different.

The primary distinction between the work of the Spirit after Pentecost is that now the major theater of activities is a community rather than isolated individuals, although the latter also occurs. Norman Snaith describes the work of the Spirit as the creation of a new fellowship, a new Messianic community. The emphasis is modified. "The test is not Abraham's sons after the flesh, but Abraham's sons according to the Spirit. The word of God is spoken in and through this fellowship, by those who believe, and by them in the power of the Holy Spirit." [66]

The community present after Pentecost is the koinonia created by the Holy Spirit. Usually this Greek word is rendered "fellowship." Nelson finds that a more basic definition is "participation in something in which others also participate." [67] Whatever be the nature of the participation, the One who creates the desire for, and the will to share in, the life of the community is none other than the Holy Spirit.

Arnold Come presents a fresh description of koinonia. He translates it as "commonwealth of the Holy Spirit." "Common" presupposes the idea of personal involvement, of sharing, while at the same time avoiding the suggestion of static impersonality. "Wealth" is intended to preserve the source of life in the community as that of the Holy Spirit. "God dwells in the midst of this people, and so makes a people out of those who were no people, by the power of his presence as Holy Spirit, Sovereign Person." [68] But the wealth which creates the community is for the sake of the church's mission of reconciliation.

Since the church is the community of the Holy Spirit, the source of the church's life is spiritual rather than sociopsychological. This must be said even though small groups without any professed relationship with the church have made significant contributions for understanding group process. To find oneself accepted when acceptance was not anticipated can be an exhilarating experience. Nevertheless, there ought to be no attempt to equate any kind of social acceptance with the spiritual dynamics present where people intend to be open to the Holy Spirit. Shoemaker is again helpful. " People who work with ' group dynamics ' may reproduce something that very much resembles the unity of the Spirit, but unless they seek the Spirit consciously and in faith, I think they may mistake the human phenomenon of enjoying the ' herdwarmth ' of human acquiescence in a psychological trend, for the real unity of the Holy Spirit. This cannot be manipulated." [69]

The church as the community of the Holy Spirit implies further that God is dynamically present. If he is present, then everything that has been predicted of the church is true for all-sized gatherings of God's people. Where they come together in Christ's name to be nurtured in the wider dimensions of this confession, the Spirit abides, infusing and informing the group. Obviously, this has nothing to do with meeting in a building designated by the municipality as " church." The church as a Spirit-filled community exists in any place where people acknowledge that they are Christ's church without denying that privilege to another fellowship similarly called. In this special community, the Holy Spirit acts to motivate people to want to learn the concerns of the Spirit and to accept him as teacher. If anything is clear in the book of The Acts it is that mighty learning experiences occurred as people were present in this new fellowship. For example, they learned the meaning of Jesus Christ in the economy of redemption (Acts 3:32-33) ; the will to share (Acts 4:31-32) ; a life of openness to the Spirit (Acts 11:12) ; and a transformation of self, which could then accept the Gentiles as persons also beloved of God (Acts 10:44-45) . Menoud's conclusion must form part of any theory of learning which purports to be adequate for Christian nurture. " He [the Holy Spirit] is a power who acts within the framework which this power has built. There alone can the spiritual life of the believer be nourished and developed." [70]

## The Holy Spirit

Mrs. Cully describes the Holy Spirit as the critical factor in Christian communication. "Education may lead people to Christ but the Holy Spirit, in his own time, will make a person aware of the One in whose presence he stands." [71] Bernard Ramm identifies the inner testimony of the Holy Spirit with intuitive rather than with discursive reasoning. Intuition is understood as the "direct apprehension of something as true, and not a conclusion at the end of a short or long chain of reasoning." [72] Bruner makes no claim for the operation of the Holy Spirit in intuitive thinking, but he invites research to determine how intuitive gifts may be developed.[73] This suggests the legitimate place for the nonanalytical in nurture.

According to the plan of procedure adopted for this chapter, there will again be an exposition of key sentences describing the Holy Spirit. Each summary section will be concluded with relevant implications for Christian nurture.

1. *The Holy Spirit is the life of God for man.*

The word for "spirit" in Hebrew is *ruach*. Its root meaning is to breathe out through the nostrils with great violence. According to Snaith, when the word is used in the Old Testament, three emphases are apparent. "It stands for power, for life, and it is of God as against man." [74]

*Ruach* is the destructive, strong, and violent wind that sweeps down through Mesopotamia from the northern mountains to the overheated gulf of the south (Ezek. 1:4). At other times, *ruach* refers to the violent energy of God in judgment (Isa. 30:28). The concept of power in *ruach* often denotes the dominant impulse that gains the ascendancy in an individual (Ex. 35:21).[75] In Job 32:18, Elihu indicates that his *ruach* requires him to speak. Again "the *ruach* is regarded as being part of the man himself, the controlling element in him, the active and determining man." [76]

When " power " and " man " come together, the implicit meaning of spirit as power becomes explicit as life through the working of God. Snaith finds Ezekiel's vision of the dry bones as the most effective context of *ruach.* God's Spirit will come from the four winds, but this will result in life rather than destruction.[77]

In the New Testament, the life-creative Spirit of the Lord is evident as related in the birth narratives. The Spirit causes the conception of Jesus in the womb of the Virgin Mary. When Jesus enters upon his formal ministry following baptism, the descent of the Spirit upon him probably is meant to show that this is the same Spirit with which the prophets were inspired. John bears witness to the life-giving Spirit in his report of the meeting of Jesus and Nicodemus. There is a birth into ordinary life that ceases at death, and there is birth into eternal life that cannot be challenged by death because the Holy Spirit is present in the believer.

It is legitimate to describe the Spirit as involved in the full dimensions of life because he is essentially life rather than an impersonal force or influence. Consequently, the Holy Spirit must be " he " instead of " it." He is always God himself, the third mode of being of the Trinity. Just as God is both personal and Holy Spirit, so he deals with man as person and as spirit. Hendry writes of the importance of understanding the Spirit as personal. " Without the personal work of the Spirit we could have Christ only as an impersonal memory. It is the living person of God, present in his Spirit, that unites us with Christ and through him deals personally with us." [78]

We may also approach the Holy Spirit as the life of God in relationship to the " spirit " of man. Emphasis upon man as spirit is not intended to pose a dichotomy. Man is body. Man is spirit. Neither can be separated from the other. But man is most assuredly spirit. Were this not the case, there would be nothing " in " man to which the Holy Spirit could relate.

Hendry distinguishes between *dependence* and *relation*. Man shares dependence on God with all creation, but man's personal relation to God can only be known at the level of the spirit. The human spirit is the organ of encounter with the Spirit of God.[79] Snaith, too, supports the idea of the divine Spirit being in correspondence with the human spirit. He sees Paul as using " spirit " as the directing power in man (Rom. 1:9; Gal. 6:18). This is not man's intellectual and moral nature. Paul is thinking in terms of the Hebrew *ruach*. As such, man's spirit is in relation to the Spirit of God. True wisdom must be received by the spiritual rather than the natural faculties. " Man as man cannot know these things." [80]

In terms of learning theory, the Holy Spirit as the life of God for man means that the concerns of Christian nurture must be learned by spiritual beings. Spirit and nonspirit are incompatible entities. Consequently, learning theories that treat man only as animal can be but partially adequate for the learning problems of the Christian faith.

These problems reflect man's body-spirit nature. Man may learn history. He may perceive human relationships with understanding. He may learn skills for life in the visible community. He may learn attitudes and values that command respect in the councils of men. All of these, however, do not add up to complete learning in the sense of Christian nurture. They are relevant learnings for man as body.

Man as spirit must learn the things of the Spirit through the life of God as Spirit. Now knowledge, understandings, attitudes, values, skills, motives, and acceptance of the self in relation to God are learned in the Spirit or they are not learned at all.

2. *The Holy Spirit leads into all truth as it is in Jesus Christ.*

Hendry takes a chronological approach to the study of the Holy Spirit. He sees the Spirit from within the experience of the primitive church rather than through antecedents of the Spirit in Israel. The Holy Spirit is always "a gift in the context of the mission and work of Christ." [81]

Jesus must be understood as the fulfillment of the Old Testament prophecy of the future outpouring of the Holy Spirit. In the descending dove at baptism, Jesus is revealed as the permanent bearer of the Spirit. The Spirit will labor through the divine unveiling in Christ. John writes that Jesus will send the Holy Spirit to the disciples. Hendry takes this as an indication that the Spirit is always *after* Christ in the divine economy. "This is because the work of the Spirit is essentially of a reproductive nature: it has always to do with the work of the incarnate Christ. . . . The Spirit is to be remembrancer, . . . not innovator." [82] Without the Spirit's interpretation, the supreme event of history could never have been perceived. The cross required the Holy Spirit to reveal the glory of God in it to the disciples.[83] For Snaith, there are two paramount interpretations of the Spirit in John's Gospel. *Paraklētos* should be translated "convictor" rather than the traditional "comforter." "The Holy Spirit is not that Spirit which comforts the disciples after the Lord Jesus has been glorified, but rather that Spirit which convinces them of the truth of the things of Christ." [84] Instead of rendering the Greek *to pneuma tes alētheias* (the Spirit of truth), Snaith prefers "Spirit of reliability, faith, or even the Spirit which creates faith." [85]

Hendry discerns that for Paul too, there is a close relationship between Spirit and Christ. "The Spirit is the subjective complement or counterpart of the objective fact of Christ, and it is the function of the Spirit to bring about an inner experience of the outward fact in the hands of men. . . . Only the Spirit can open the door to a real, inner apprehension of the Lordship of Christ." [86] In other words, to know Christ is to know him from God's point of view, and this is impossible for man. If man is to recognize who God is and to respond to him, the initiative must be God's.

Such recognition and response follows from the Spirit's convicting man of his sin and leading him to repentance. In Paul's great chapter on the Holy Spirit (Rom., ch. 8), he assures the Christian that life may indeed continue in trial and tribulation, but at the same time he is a new creation. Now the challenges of faith are placed in their proper perspective. They do not have the final word. Through the Holy Spirit, Christ's victory is perceived as real and henceforth nothing can separate the believer from the love of God. The "fruit of the Spirit" (Gal. 5:22) is also evidence of the Spirit's transforming the believer through applying the redemption wrought by Christ. A degree of love, joy, peace, and patience, for example, may be attained through human striving. But Paul anticipates that these qualities are more unique than similar virtues discussed by Greek philosophers. Paul's learning of joy and peace is the result of God's grace through the orientation of the Holy Spirit.[87]

If the Holy Spirit leads into all truth as it is in Jesus Christ, then this implies that Christian nurture is bound by the character of the revelation of God in Christ. The nature of the revelation determines what is to be learned. This suggests, too, that the foundation for learning in the Christian community is given in the task of the Holy Spirit. As he does his work in the world with reference to God's redemptive act in Christ, so the things related to Christ must be learned in the Spirit.

Through the Holy Spirit, man learns that he is a sinner. Objectively, man may learn that something is amiss with himself. Any casual reading of the daily newspaper must remove any doubt about his condition. However, only the

Holy Spirit can take these feelings of bewilderment, uneasiness, disgust, and transform them into convictions of sin as estrangement from God and from one another.

The reality of the encounter between Jesus Christ and the learner is also due to the power of the Holy Spirit. Persons may structure situations so that there is study of the Scriptures, but the Holy Spirit alone may effect the learning.

Through the Holy Spirit, learners came to reassess and change their understandings, attitudes, values, and motives. Through the Spirit, weak men have learned to rely on God. In this reliance, they have become uncommonly strong. Something beyond human insight was necessary to change the cross from a symbol of defeat into a symbol of victory. The transformation of the response to the symbol resulted in a complete relearning of value. Instead of value being identified with a study of the law, value was found in bearing witness to a living Lord. Instead of the attitude of impulsive judgment which would call down the fire of God on offenders, there was the attitude of love in the *agapē* sense. Instead of the motive of self-preservation that could result in a denial of the Lord, there was the learned motive of committed discipleship and that without reservation. "Whether it is right in the sight of God to listen to you rather than to God, you must judge; for we cannot but speak of what we have seen and heard." (Acts 4:19-20.) Instead of the Scriptures speaking of a future deliverance, new understanding was learned that the Scriptures were now fulfilled in Christ.

When the apostles attempted to explain what had happened to them, no more adequate terminology was available than to speak of their experience as being brought from death to life or being born from above or being newly created. These terms indicate the most profound transformation of the self. It is a transformation that cannot be accounted for by the conditioning stimuli of the cultural milieu or the attainment of happiness or the aggressive outreach of an active intellect. Combs and Snygg ask whether one can conceive of the kind of world that might result were it possible to find release from " the slavery of inadequate concepts of self." [88] It is the peculiar vocation of the Holy Spirit to answer such a question of self-transformation in its ultimate sense. To speak of the Holy Spirit in this way is by no means to shift attention away from legitimate human action. It is to clear away much confusion in Christian nurture by asserting that the goal of changed persons is a possibility only within dynamic action by the Holy Spirit as he brings persons to affirmative decisions for Jesus Christ. Changed selves are the work of the Holy Spirit.

3. *The Holy Spirit is God's freedom to act.*

In the Old Testament, the Spirit is a manifestation of God's creative power. He is said to have brooded over the watery waste before the earth and life came into existence. (Gen. 1:2.) Joseph's stewardship in Egypt is described as the result of the indwelling of the Spirit of God. In other words, God was working out his purposes through Joseph as one receptive to the Spirit. (Gen. 41:38.) The Spirit descended on certain individuals such as the prophets and the servant of the Lord to empower them to proclaim the word which must be spoken and the deed which must be accomplished. (Micah 3:8; Isa. 42:1; Isa. 61:1.) Menoud writes that in short " in the old covenant, the Spirit intervenes sporadically by quickening the men upon whom devolved the responsibility of leading Israel towards her providential destiny." [89]

But the Spirit can never be compelled to act. Jesus likens the operation of the Spirit to the action of the wind blowing where it wills. (John 3:8.) Henry P. Van Dusen summarizes the history of the church as the " pathetic and tragic story " of the Holy Spirit's struggle to remain free. Church authorities, Roman Catholic and Protestant, are charged with the attempt to bind the Spirit and to render him impotent. "But the Holy Spirit has always been troublesome, disturbing because it has seemed to be unruly, radical, unpredictable. It is always embarrassing to ecclesiasticism and baffling to ethically grounded, responsible, durable Christian devotion. . . . When neglected or denied by the prevailing 'churchianity,' it unfailingly reappears to reassert its power, often with excesses and aberrations, beyond the bounds of conventional church life." [90] It is not a matter of accident, so Van Dusen believes, that the nineteenth-century missionary advance was accomplished primarily through Christian groups which came directly out of Radical Protestantism, such as the Baptists, Methodists, and Moravians.[91]

As God's freedom to act, the Holy Spirit reminds men to repent and turn away from all closed systems and false philosophies that leave no place for the living God. Repentance means turning to him in faith. Life's orientation now permits the inclusion of the nonstructured as also normal. But more important, man is emancipated from the rigid cause-and-effect relationships which have been both his support and his prison. Because events issue in certain effects, man finds security in trying to control his environment. But when he becomes so entangled in the skeins of his passion for ordered structures, his perceptual processes permit him to see but limited horizons. The Spirit gives man back his liberty as man. Tournier has rightly noted that "the Spirit . . . frees us completely from the natural mechanisms by which we have hitherto been determined." [92]

If the Holy Spirit really is God's freedom to act, there must be caution in all attempts to develop self-contained systems without regard to his presence. This includes learning theory in general and its application to the needs of the Christian faith.

A theory of learning for Christian nurture ceases to be helpful once learning is reduced to a series of explanations without regard to the operation of the Holy Spirit. Learning theory has then fallen back upon the capacity of man to master every aspect of his destiny. Just here, an explanation for learning the deeper things of the faith has ceased. This does not mean that learning theory ought to be chaotic. But it is a reminder that theory ought to be flexible and open to the Holy Spirit. He determines whether there has been nurture or general learning.

It is also as unfortunate to have the Holy Spirit inserted in learning theory as an afterthought as it is to have him omitted completely. He belongs at the heart of the theory. To say that the Spirit makes all concerns possible does not treat the problem seriously. Such an approach suggests that the Holy Spirit is unnecessary until the time comes to authenticate human insight. Because it is difficult to define the Holy Spirit operationally, he is relegated to an insignificant place in the day-to-day aspects of Christian nurture where learning is expressed at the level of instruction. If the Holy Spirit is the effector of learning in Christian nurture, then provision must be made for his action at every point in the learning process.

Because the Holy Spirit is the freedom of God, each implication drawn from theology thus far is dependent upon the initiative of the Holy Spirit to confront persons with Christ. In the persisting relationship with the Spirit, the human perceptive processes are so guided that the person comes to learn at the most fundamental point open to him — change in the self.

The teachings of the four doctrines — revelation, man, the church, and the Holy Spirit — have a tendency to converge at various points. This is as it should be since God's work in man's behalf cannot be held in mutually exclusive compartments. But it does not mean that any one doctrine would be sufficiently comprehensive in itself to provide the necessary theological foundations for learning theory. Nor does it mean that the theological understanding of process could be subsumed under either revelation or the Holy

Spirit, for example. Revelation is the freedom of God in disclosing himself to perceiving selves in terms of the Biblical drama of salvation. God cannot be compelled to reveal, and all human striving will not alter this basic fact, although the likelihood of revelation may be increased by letting oneself be available to what God is about to do. At the same time, there is no revelation without the Holy Spirit, yet the Holy Spirit is distinct from revelation. The Holy Spirit is God himself creating new selves through the totality of man's relationships but in particular through the redemption wrought in Christ.

Similarities and distinctions are also evident when man is studied through the Biblical witness and as he is in community. Man is God's covenant partner, as is the church. But the church is more than an organization of individuals. There is a corporateness about the church which expresses a life greater than that indicated by specific living individuals. The nurture of which man is capable is only fully realized as he is bound up within the fellowship of God's people.

How these theological insights may be expressed for the evaluation of learning theory and for the outlining of a possible theory for Christian nurture will be the subject of the following chapters.

## Chapter V

# A Theological Evaluation of Learning Theory

Thus far in this investigation, learning theory and the theological foundations have been pursued independently of each other. There have been momentary occasions when they have approached a relationship, but there has been no genuine dialogue. Now the place has been reached where the two disciplines may be brought together through an assessment of theological validity of the various learning theories.

The problem of dialogue issuing in theological validity is a difficult one. Theology and learning theory are disparate disciplines. Their methodologies and presuppositions are in contrast.

Christian theology is based on revealed truth. This is hardly to claim that the theology of a particular theologian is identical with revelation! It is, however, to assert that the basic theological insights come into space time from beyond space time. The life of the invisible God becomes incarnate in Jesus Christ.

Substantively, revelation is the foundation of Christian theology. But theological formulations are not expressed in the form of revelation. They are developed as Barth has said by " a laborious advance from one partial human insight to another, intending but by no means guaranteeing an ' advance.' "[1] Theology utilizes all of the intellectual faculties necessary for any human work. Indeed, it is impossible to escape the cultural imprint on theology. H. Richard Niebuhr's observation must not be forgotten:

"Man not only speaks but thinks with the aid of the language of culture." [2] Therefore, theology's methodology includes such tools of culture as language study; scrutiny of the past and present documents of the church, their comparison, analysis, and evaluation. Research is conducted with reasonable objectivity. No particular conclusion is predetermined. Yet theology is never able to escape its basic presupposition that truth is neither a human invention nor discovery. Truth has entered the human sphere in Jesus Christ. This truth is perceived as theologians pursue their work within the church and not outside of it. Within the framework of the "givenness" of revelation and the context of the church, theologians are not only free but are under obligation to determine the meaning of God's continuing revelation in Jesus Christ for the faith and life of the present.

Learning theory as a science knows of no "givenness" other than those orderly sequences implied in causality. Without controlled procedures, no scientific theories would be possible. Orderliness is the basis for the repeatability of experiments. Poincaré states that the methodology of science "rests on the induction which makes us expect the repetition of a phenomenon when the circumstances under which it first happened are reproduced." [3] If the learning-theory experiment under study is correct, the same results should be obtained by other researchers using the same conditions expressed in the original study. When a sufficient number of experiments have realized identical results, the theory is said to be confirmed. As in all induction, there is no certainty about the number of experiments necessary to justify a valid generalization. It becomes a subjective decision. If a conclusion has been reached, and another experiment issues in contrary results, it becomes necessary to go over the study again. Further experiments are devised and the quest for inductive verification is continued. As a matter of method, learning theory designs tests to check one or two elements in a larger whole while maintaining other variables constant. Even a cursory examination of learning-theory reports in *The Psychological Review* makes this methodology apparent. Through such objectification, learning as a field of inquiry lays claim to being a science.

For all of learning theory's emphases upon quantifiable results, it is inaccurate to say that it has no nonquantifiable presuppositions. In the first place, learning theory as a science makes the assumption that dependable knowledge must be gained through rigid experimentation. W. J. Brogden gives evidence of this mind set when he writes: "Empirical observation of one's dog, one's children, one's fellows, one's client, one's self have no place in the construction of theory, nor is their use legitimate in arguments that purport to favor or oppose a given theory. A scientific theory is relevant only to the facts and relations obtained by scientific methods."[4] This may be an adequate or an inadequate assumption, but it is an assumption and not a scientific conclusion. It ignores evidence that cannot be easily objectified. The first assumption leads into a second. Because controlled situations can be devised for lower animals in ways not possible for humans, it is assumed that there is a continuity between lower and higher animal forms. However, this has not been demonstrated. It is a working hypothesis.

Now how may theology grounded in revelation, and learning theory based on scientific experimentation be brought together? How can one of two such different fields of study validate the conclusions of the other?

If validation means that theology is to determine whether the conclusion of a learning-theory experiment with white rats is true, then validation is neither possible in itself nor is it a responsible goal. Theological validation has no part in ascertaining the truth of experimental evidence. But it does have a vocation for study of the implications which, learning theory concludes, follow from the experiment. For example, conditioning is without doubt a valid description of how some learning occurs. It is not a foregone conclusion, however, that conditioning is the principal way people learn. Neither is it necessarily true that conditioning is an appropriate base on which to develop learning tasks for Christian nurture. Therefore, theological validation is the examination of learning-theory conclusions to see if they possess theological integrity for the concerns of Christian nurture.[5]

Since theological validation cannot mean the confirmation of experimental data, a common ground between theology and learning theory must be found for which the process of validation is relevant. It is anticipated that such a meeting place may be determined by transposing the four theological doctrines discussed into issues of equal concern to both learning theory and theology. The approach to the common concerns is by way of theology rather than learning theory because the four doctrines impose manageable limitations on the articulation of mutual issues. To transpose learning-theory categories into problems common to it and theology would be more unwieldy because learning theory as an expanding science is less precise than theology. The content of theological doctrines varies with each generation's attempt to express the message of the church, but the categories are relatively stable because of the nature of revelation.

The application of the theological foundations as norms for evaluating the general character of the particular learning theory will be given after the common concerns have been specified. Later, there will be a comparable theological assessment of each learning theory's answers to the representative concerns to be learned in Christian nurture.

## Determination of Common Concerns

### 1. *Revelation and Learning Theory*

At first consideration, there appear to be no concerns common to revelation and learning theory. Revelation is grounded in God, and God is not a learning-theory category. However, if revelation is understood as a single event that includes the divine initiative and the human response, a clue is given for establishing a common point of meeting between revelation and learning theory. This fact of equal interest to both disciplines is *the recurrence of human responses consistent with the presence of certain stimuli.*

The human response is significant in Christian nurture. The learner is to be someone; he is to do something. He is to learn to be a disciple of Christ and to effect his discipleship in the world as a member of the covenant community, the body of Christ, and the fellowship of the Holy Spirit. At the deepest level of learning, the stimulus is God himself in confrontation with the learner, seeking to elicit responses such as faith, love, obedience, and service. Revelation is both the stimulus and the response. Without either, there is no personal revelation. Consequently, revelation finds itself thoroughly involved in the recurrence of responses consistent with itself.

Learning theory, whether of the stimulus-response or the cognitive type, attempts to explain how certain response patterns may be learned. Responses, broadly interpreted, are evidences of learning. Some theorists prefer to say that responses are inferences of the observer that learning has occurred. There may be learning where there is no evidence such as in the sign-gestalt experiments. Stimulus-response theorists tend to think of responses as habits due to muscular action or to the effects of reinforcement. Cognitive theorists are inclined to broaden the meaning of responses to more than muscular action because of the reflex connotations of the term in the hands of the stimulus-response theorists. Cognitive theorists place more stress upon responses of "knowing" as a necessary prelude to "doing." Organisms learn "facts," "cognitive structures," "what leads to what," and "expectancies." Whether habits or facts, learning theory would be without meaning were it not for the tendency of organisms to respond to stimuli. Therefore, learning theory is actually a science of learned responses.

2. *Man and Learning Theory*

Theology seeks to bring its insights into focus upon man as the subject of Christian nurture. Accordingly, the doctrine of man is a theological description of the human learner. This is directly suggestive of a common concern for learning theory and theology. It may be defined as *the learner in learning.*

Theology is " the science of God," but it is keenly aware of man. It never escapes its autobiographical character. Theology is a human work subject to human limitations. Yet it transcends some of those limitations as it grapples with the meaning of the nature and destiny of the visible member of the divine-human covenant. In this sense, man in relation to God is the subject of theology. Man is created in the image of God. Man is a sinner, but God does not desert him. He is called to become a member of the cast in the drama of redemption. For man's salvation, God became man. It is no wonder that theology is motivated to understand how man may perceive his basic identity. Consequently, the learner in learning is a necessary concern of theology.

Learning theory has no interest in the theological view of man, but it makes judgments about the learner. All learning theorists devise experiments appropriate to the organism's learning potential. No other course is open. Ideational concepts can be utilized with human but not subhuman subjects. At a more fundamental level, learning theorists must make a basic decision about the learner. Are the responses of the organism due to " peripheral " or to " central " intermediaries? If the choice is in favor of the peripheral, the learner is viewed as a highly modified reflex mechanism. Stimuli come to the learner and result in responses of muscular movements, such as in Guthrie's contiguous conditioning. If the presupposition is in favor of central intermediaries, the organism's brain processes carry the major load as in gestalt theory.

Although learning theory is not metaphysical, it makes metaphysical judgments about the learner whenever it determines the design of the experiments and the kind of evidence to be admitted as scientifically acceptable. The learner remains a central concern in learning theory.

### 3. *The Church and Learning Theory*

At a minimum, the church is a community of persons. At its best, the church is nothing less than a divine community. Since the church always includes the divine referent, Christian nurture is held to be questionable if not impossible outside of it. The church, therefore, suggests that another concern common to theology and learning theory is *the context of learning*.

The doctrine of the church is the attempt to understand the nature of the divine community. The church inquires whether the lofty terms predicated of it — covenant community, body of Christ, fellowship of the Holy Spirit — are of verbal interest only or whether they point to an intrinsic quality not found elsewhere. If the church is a unique community, as is held here, then it is a learning situation that communicates God's truth through what it is. There is learning due to the quality of interpersonal relationships found in its fellowship. To assert that the church's nature determines its nurture immediately involves the church in an abiding concern with the context of learning.

Learning theory does not dwell upon the context as a special category, but it is implicit in all of the theories studied. Terms are found such as "stimulus situation," "stimulus pattern," "total learning situation," and "structure." All of these have context as the one feature in common. Stimulus-response theories tend to treat specific stimuli as isolated phenomena for purposes of study. Yet the conditioning theorist does not deny that the various elements of an experiment may modify the organism's behavior. Conditioning expects to control the elements. If the larger learning situation is implicit in stimulus-response theories, it is explicit in cognitive theories. The entire learning situation is the focus of interest. In the "detour" experiments, the organism cannot solve the problem if it studies the barrier and the goal-object alone. When the organism sees the total situation of goal-object, barrier, and way-around-the-barrier as a unit, learning may occur.

### 4. *The Holy Spirit and Learning Theory*

As in revelation, the doctrine of the Holy Spirit presents a category that appears to defy any attempt to find a common ground with learning theory. The Holy Spirit in his freedom is the antithesis of scientific causality and the attempt to exercise exact control over the learning process. Stated in terms of freedom and rigidity, the quest for a common concern reaches an impasse. But if the problem is expressed as an inquiry into the power which effects learning, then a common ground is in view. This may be offered as *the dynamics of the learning process.*

Theology confesses that change in persons is ultimately not a human work at all. Persons may be guided to a revelatory situation, such as the study of John's Gospel. They may comprehend the principal members of the dramatic event under discussion, but the gap between preparatory learning and real learning has not necessarily been closed. It remains for the Holy Spirit to apply the Biblical insights to the human need, and thereby effect change in the person. The Holy Spirit is the One who leads persons to desire to learn of God and to accept the cost of discipleship. In a word, the Holy Spirit in theology involves Christian nurture in a consideration of the dynamics of the learning process.

Learning theory has no category of Holy Spirit. However, it must deal with the question of the dynamics of learning. Among stimulus-response theorists, this factor is usually described as motivation. The organism acts to reduce a tension, to escape from pain, or to achieve a satisfying state of affairs. At other times, an intervening variable or a hypothetical construct is posited as the critical factor between the stimulus and the resulting response. An intervening variable has been defined as "an inferred relationship between the independent variable (stimulus) and the dependent variable (response)."[6] It is considered a functional necessity for the theory. If the variable is held to be quantifiable, it may be called a "hypothetical construct." Later research may identify the construct. If this is the case, its hypothetical character is removed. But whether intervening variable or hypothetical construct, "something" provides the motive power or force for learning.

Cognitive theorists utilize the foregoing concepts as well but dwell less upon motivation as the result of the organism's need states. The dynamics of learning are centered more in the learner himself — his active intellect, his perception of the situation — and the field of force generated within the total learning context, that is, the learner, the goal, and their mutual interaction.

Whether the answers of the stimulus-response or the cognitive theorists are preferred, learning theory in general makes critical judgments about the dynamics of learning.

Four common concerns have been noted to which theology and learning theory may bring their insights: the recurrence of human responses consistent with the stimuli, the learner in learning, the context of learning, and the dynamics of learning.

## A Theological Evaluation of Four Learning Theories

Each learning theory is to be examined in turn. In so far as possible, one terse statement will be stated for the particular learning theory's answer to the common concern. This is followed by a reflection of the answer in the light of the theological norms established.

### 1. *Reinforcement Theory and Theology*

*Responses that have become connected with certain stimuli through the learner's trial-and-error behavior will always be elicited when those stimuli are re-presented under similar conditions.*

In the basic frame of reference, the stimuli are viewed as external to the learner. In its more refined expression, reinforcement theory permits internal stimuli for learning.

There can be no theological disagreement with the concomitance of stimuli and responses as the foundation of learning. The tendency to respond to stimuli permits God to reach persons. It is this fact which is the human condition for revelation. As the Incarnate Word, Jesus came to persons anticipating that his presence would evoke some kind of response. His coming did cause reactions. From some he received the response of indifference, from some the response of hostility, and from a minority the response of grateful love.

To acknowledge the centrality of responses in human life is not the same as accepting the interpretation of stimuli and responses in reinforcement theory, however. In so far as stimulus-response connections become established through random trials until the proper solution is realized, reinforcement is theologically valid. It reflects the creaturely order as planned by God. But to the degree that trial-and-error learning is considered the prototype for modifying all behavior, it is invalid. The theological understanding of revelation holds to a disclosure by God rather than to a random searching after him. To be sure, man may search after God and satisfying experiences with him may encourage continued seeking, but it is not the reinforcement which ultimately issues in experiencing God. The Father comes to man first.

Furthermore, all learning of God is not necessarily " satisfying " as this term is usually interpreted. Knowing God often involves the knower in actions that genuinely try his soul. Again, the theological view of revelation does not hold to the position that the stimulus and the response are two isolated events that become connected under reinforcement. Revelation conceives of the stimulus and the response as a unity. God addresses the human understanding in order to elicit a response, but he empowers man to respond. Therefore, reinforcement's answer to the problem of responses becoming connected with stimuli is both theologically sound in certain respects and invalid in others.

*The learner is an active being co-extensive with nature and to be understood through objective analysis.*

In reinforcement theory, man is not qualitatively different from lower organisms. Principles of learning appropriate for the laboratory animal are considered equally true for human learning. In both cases, the learner acts in response to the presented stimuli by engaging in unproductive behavior before the problem is mastered. On subsequent occasions, the problem is solved with less wasted effort if the behavior was rewarded. Accordingly, the basic evidence of learning is the habit — the regular occurrence of action related to a specific stimulus or stimulus situation. It is also held that a basic knowledge of learning may be determined by observation of the subject-organism. His own view of the test is not critical.

The expressed action corresponds with the phylogenetic level of the organism. On this scale, man's responses are admittedly more refined. His mental faculties permit him to differentiate from among a variety of cues. While man is able to reason, the fundamental process is not altered. Responses produce other verbal and instrumental cues that in turn evoke other responses until the behavior is learned. Thinking is a more advanced end-product in a complicated chain of stimuli and responses. It is not considered necessary to assume that higher mental processes require the elaboration of any construct such as the self. Man as a learner remains within a behavioristic framework.

The Christian doctrine of man is agreeable with analyses of man at the biological level. Reinforcement theory is considered valid for describing the human learner where acquisition of physical skills and habits is the learning goal. Before actions judged as skills become so in fact, numerous trials are made. The unrewarded responses tend to be reduced in number while the ones rewarded persist until the action proceeds smoothly. Through reinforcement studies, man is reminded of his relationships with other creatures. This is part of the doctrine of man and theologically valid.

However, when more is claimed for reinforcement theory, theology must dissent. The Christian view of man cannot accept the behavioristic man as the real man. Through revelation and personal reflection, man perceives himself as a transcendent being. In revelation he is known as a self who comprehends his identity in relationship with the Self who is God. Furthermore, as a covenant partner of God, man is known as a responsible being with an internal life worthy of consideration. He is not a helpless being who must engage in random action before accidentally arriving at the right solution. The mature man grasps the total situation and chooses the response most consonant with its demands. He will not be fenced in by externally imposed restraints until these have become part of his self-structure and necessary for his own self-integrity. Man in response to the call of God must frequently be the rebel against the status quo. Hence, to be a man is to be bound more by freedom than by necessity. There is little place for the free response to God and the consequent refusal to be limited absolutely by cultural restraints in the "reinforcement man."

Theology sees Jesus Christ as God, yes, but also as truly man. Can he be compressed into the reinforcement paradigm? On the basis of the New Testament reports, Jesus is portrayed as an individual who grew in wisdom and who was motivated by more than drive reduction. The one experience of childhood related by the Gospel writers should have issued in a discontinuance of learning if reinforcement is unquestionably correct. Instead of receiving the reinforcement of praise for his conduct in the Temple, Jesus is rebuked by his mother. He should have soliloquized his " pain " by saying, " I am not worthy of my mother's trust; I have failed." Instead we read, " Did you not know that I must be in my Father's house? " (Luke 2:49b.) In his interpersonal relations, Jesus is portrayed as one who is able to penetrate to the heart of the matter. He perceives relationships directly and without coming to an insight through numerous experiences of reward and nonreward.

On the basis of man in relationship with other creatures, reinforcement theory is theologically valid. Where there is a discontinuity between man and the creatures as is evident in the revelation of man in Jesus Christ, reinforcement theory is invalid.

*The context of learning is the organism with its need state and the stimulus of an unfamiliar situation which together evoke two or more responses.*

The need state is usually defined as tissue needs such as food, water, sex, and escape from noxious stimuli. Secondary need states are more important for man. He learns not only how and where to find food, but how and where to find a particular kind. A need state for an intellectual problem may be the anticipation of personal betterment. For this reason, persons may persist in the temporary sacrifices necessary to achieve advanced education in the expectation of greater status and financial security.

By linking the organism's need state and an unfamiliar situation, reinforcement theory emphasizes that the learner and the situation belong together. Learning occurs in a permissive environment. The learner is not forced to learn before it is ready. No buzzer is heard and no shocks are received! Furthermore, the stimulus pattern is so arranged that the learner is free to seek out the correct solution. While human trial-and-error learning may be conducted in co-operation with other persons, these are relatively unnecessary. The permissive atmosphere encourages individual rather than group exploration.

The theological doctrines of man and the church permit a partial validation of reinforcement's answer to the context of learning. Readiness as a prerequisite to learning is a Thorndikian discovery, but it is related to the Christian doctrine of man. Beginning with creation, there has been a patient waiting for man by God. Man is not commanded to respond. God takes the initiative in redemption and man is to receive the proffered gift. The fullness of man does not happen in one instant of time. Man becomes man through gradual transformation. In terms of learning, man may receive guidance appropriate to his capacities and interests.

The free stimulus situation in which there may be trial and error, exploration and discovery is valid according to the church's nature as the redemptive community. In this permissive environment, problems may be defined and solutions discerned at the learner's pace.

The concept of readiness is related to tissue needs in the learner and has been judged as theologically valid. Genuine needs of the learner are part of the context of learning. However, the doctrine of man cannot permit an unqualified endorsement of readiness. Concentration on the learner's needs may result in a subtle shift of emphasis until he is being controlled by the educator. At the same time, building a theory of learning upon needs presupposes that the educator is fully competent to determine what the learner's needs are; it anticipates equally the learner's ability to delineate his true condition now and in the future. But if the learner knows his needs, what of the vocation of the church as covenant community? The church is responsible to God for the communication of the offer of covenant and the heritage of faith. This involves an awareness of the true need of the learner rather than that which he may consider significant. From another perspective, readiness is less acceptable theologically. As indicating a tissue need, readiness would mean that the possibility of encounter with God exists at the biological level alone. The Christian doctrine of man, to the contrary, knows nothing of a drive state for God in order to maintain a tissue balance. It knows only of a self addressed by God. In the encounter, the response involves the total self and not just the organic self.

The permissive stimulus situation implicit in trial-and-error learning is valid, but it presupposes that the learner must always be engaged in searching behavior. No provision is made for the self to completely restructure the stimulus situation without any trial and error. If the operation of the Holy Spirit has validity within the church, then there must be provision for suddenness of perception in learning under the Holy Spirit.

Again, context as determined in reinforcement theory must be judged as but partially valid because it provides no necessary function for other persons. These may be involved as part of the stimulus situation, but the trial-and-error action is an individual matter. The Christian revelation indicates that the truth of God is mediated through persons in the dialogue of mutual address and response. To be theologically valid, the context of learning must make provision for the centrality of community in which revelation is heard. Learning theory does not, of course, need to use the word " church " to be valid. Yet it must provide for a community of learning because man learns to know himself in relationship with at least one person and God.

*The dynamics of learning is reinforcement, since learning occurs only as a tension is reduced, a drive is lessened, a problem is solved, or a satisfaction is obtained.* In substance, without reward, people do not learn.

Learners, whether infrahuman or human, have a tendency to repeat experiences that were previously rewarding. This commonsense observation is corroborated by unimpeachable experimental evidence. It is related to the concern for wholeness of the individual in the doctrine of man. Theological foundations, then, can accept the dynamics of reinforcement as valid because it is appropriate for man as a physical organism.

If the concept of reinforcement is valid, there must yet be inquiry whether any aspect of the theological understanding of revelation and man may render it inadvisable as the theoretical foundation for developing learning tasks in Christian nurture. A judicious use of verbalized rewards facilitates interpersonal relations and would appear to increase the possibility for the divine revelation to be mediated by persons. An absence of any reinforcing situation could lead to a breakdown of relationships between persons. However, learning theory in Christian nurture based on the principle of reward must proceed with great caution. Rewards can be pursued for their own sakes and consequently become interposed between God and man. Where rewards get in the way of revelation, reinforcement theory becomes theologically invalid.

As an interpreter of the life of the church, theology must raise a further question. Is reinforcement an incontestable law of learning for all purposes? The church conceives itself to be a covenant community with the sense of responsibility implied in such a society. Can the church learn responsibility according to reinforcement dynamics? For responsibility to be learned, it is necessary to make the assumption that actions considered responsible bring on a reduction of tension or the satisfaction of drives. However, more often than not, responsibility within the covenant community requires actions which may issue in pain rather than pleasure, death rather than life. According to the dynamics of reinforcement theory, nonrewarded behavior should be discontinued. This is not true for Christian responsibility. Mrs. Cully has placed the problem in proper focus through her criticism of some methods of teaching the experience of " taking turns " to kindergarten children. There may be informal play and a story illustrating the idea. But as Mrs. Cully writes, " Such a session nowhere faces the fact that taking turns may not be fun." [7] This is the crucial point. To learn the acceptance of duty may increase rather than lessen tension.

Were reinforcement theory accepted as the *sine qua non* of learning in the church, there would be a denial of the central dynamic of Christian nurture. The Holy Spirit applies the life, ministry, death, resurrection, and abiding presence of Christ to the believers. It is the Holy Spirit who determines whether persons learn of God or merely about God. In brief, the church cannot have it both ways. It may not have learning by reinforcement only and still be serious about the necessity of the Holy Spirit in its life.

2. *Conditioning Theory and Theology*

*Responses become connected with certain stimuli through a single combination of conditioned stimuli and responses.*

The definition given reflects the behavioristic orientation of conditioning. Stimuli effect responses through the peripheral nervous system. In this, conditioning is similar to reinforcement theory. There is also a difference. Conditioning is more rigid in its approach to the relationship between stimuli and responses. Stimuli can be controlled to elicit the desired reactions. In reinforcement theory, responses are made and abandoned unless they result in reward.

From the norm of revelation, another meaning is given responses. Instead of action, which must occur in the presence of stimuli, there is found an element of uncertainty. The stimulus of God, seeking to disclose himself does not automatically result in the response of love. There is no assurance that a divine-human encounter will result at a particular moment no matter how often a response was made to God on prior occasions of a similar type.

This means conditioning is theologically invalid in its interpretation of responses to the degree they are held to occur through necessity. Conditioning prefers not to deal with responses as functions of a free, determining self. However, in so far as human learning operates at the reflex level, conditioning is theologically valid.

*The learner is a reactive being co-extensive with nature and to be understood through objective analysis.*

Knowledge of man as learner obtained through other than laboratory-controlled situations is of no interest to conditioning except for illustrative purposes. Man is an organism closely related to other mammals. His mental faculties make it possible for him to live a more refined existence, but this does not mean a self-structure needs to be postulated. Man may be comprehended within a naturalistic continuum.

Theology appreciates the conclusions of conditioning theory, concerning man's tendency to react. As a creature, man shares in mechanisms that make life possible. Man could not survive were he not the reactive creature. In the presence of noxious stimuli, man is stimulated to withdraw to more congenial surroundings. This is the theological validity of generalizing human learning from experiment with animals involving charged grids, frightening sounds, and food dispensing devices. Accordingly, the learner in conditioning has integrity to the extent that man is a reactive creature.

Theology goes beyond man in the image of animals to man in the image of God. As God's representative on earth living in relationship, man is called to responsible existence. It is impossible to find a place for human accountability if man's basic characteristic is reactive. Man is then compelled to react in a way consonant with the stimuli. The free response-in-love to God is out of the realm of possibility. Again, if man is reactive, there is no provision for either purpose or cognitively designated goals.

According to the theological view of man, he is seen as moved more by internal choice than by external manipulation. He is free to step beyond himself to become both the knower and the known. In brief, he is a conscious self with an interior life of his own. To accept conditioning would be to acquiesce in the validity of objectively handling one self by another. If man is a self, he cannot be controlled, bound, pushed, or stimulated by another without his full consent. Man is never object theologically. He is always subject.

Conditioning is theologically valid for describing the learner as a habit creature. It is invalid in its epistemology and its failure to provide for the learner as responsible and purposive.

*The context of learning is the peripheral nervous system of the learner, the conditioned stimuli, and the educator.*

All of these are present as the " place " where learning occurs. The educator is understood as a person or as the cultural milieu in which the learner lives. In the latter case, the control over learning is unconscious. It is the way the culture impresses its values and perspectives on its members. Certain persons, facts, or events produce reactions. When labels are attached to these, the labels are empowered to produce the same reaction as the original fact.

The cultural milieu must be considered as part of the stimulus situation, but for purposes of formal learning the educator is the individual teacher. He is responsible for eliciting the correct responses. He does not wait for learners to respond at their leisure. Hence, conditioning has the possibility of greater efficiency in learning. The wasted effort typical of reinforcement theory is avoided.

Conditioning is experimentally and functionally true. Since this is based on the way man is constituted as a creature, theology accepts conditioning as a valid description of the context in learning. It is also part of the functional life of the church. The immature members are unconsciously conditioned to the value orientation of the church as it is first encountered in the family. Here the child senses a feeling of love, acceptance, and well-being. When the basis of familial love is discerned as related to God, the word " God " may evoke a similar response of love. In a comparable way, the church as community conditions its members to the quality of its life. Christian nurture must also be aware of the operation of conditioning in the larger society.

Conditioning is valid as the means by which the church communicates its knowledge concerns. Instead of having each person stumble through life without assistance, conditioning permits the heritage of the community to become immediately available through a sharing of verbal symbols. Sin is both a state of humanity and a particular expression of spiritual sickness. Respect for property is discovered in other ways than through the anxiety experienced after judgment has been administered. Through conditioning, the short cut by which the community passes on its experiences to the immature, the phrase " sacredness of property " may be able to evoke the response of respect for ownership without trial-and-error learning. At this point, the context of learning in conditioning is theologically valid.

There are also aspects of conditioning which make it invalid for the life of the church. Since in conditioning, the context of learning depends thoroughly upon the educator's control of the situation, there must be a subjection of the learner's will to that of the educator. This is a violation of selfhood and therefore renders the context of conditioning theologically suspect. According to the doctrine of revelation, Christian truth is communicated through persons as the church. This is the koinonia in which God reveals himself. Conditioning misses the free address and response between educator and learner.

Again, the context of conditioning is invalid because it presupposes that learning is a matter of exercising rigid control over the stimuli which will elicit the desired responses. Such a closed context is in conflict with the freedom implicit in the operation of the Holy Spirit. He cannot be one of the stimuli under the control of the educator, and without the Holy Spirit there can be no Christian nurture at its deepest level.

*Learning occurs in a single combination of stimuli and responses through the mechanism of movement-produced stimuli.* This is the dynamic of learning in conditioning.

The actual conditioned stimuli are the peripheral nerve cells that activate muscles. Whether the subject matter is a physical or an intellectual skill, movements are learned rather than the respective skills. The learner learns what he is doing. Rewards are unimportant for the dynamics of learning; they are only of significance for what they cause the learner to do.

The dynamics of learning as movement-produced stimuli are legitimate because man is a creature with a body. Movements of that body may result in creaturely learning. Especially where physical skills are involved, physical practice is important. Learning to be a leader of worship is more than a purely verbal exercise. There is rehearsal in the setting where the skills are to be used. Movement to the lectern, standing before it, feeling the hymn book and the Bible, eye movements surveying the chapel, and the tongue movements of speech may all be presumed as factors in learning the skill of worship. In its stress on movements, the dynamics of conditioning theory are valid.

Where learning occurs primarily through encounter with God, conditioning is invalid. Were conditioning held to be valid here, there would be no theological insight of Person meeting person. Instead, there would be an unidentified Stimulus touching a reflex muscle system. Whether there may be movements in this exchange is unimportant. The " unit " in man for his reception of God is the human understanding or in physiological terms, the central rather than the peripheral nervous system. For the dynamics of any learning theory to be valid for Christian nurture, there must be provision for the full response of a self-determining person. A reflex system does not meet this qualification. Real encounter and consequently learning means not muscle movement, but the Spirit who is God being in relation with the spirit who is man.

### 3. *Gestalt Theory and Theology*

*Responses are cognitive functions of a stimulus situation.* For gestalt theory, responses do not happen automatically, as it were, they occur because of the learner's intentions. He determines the responses to be made as required by the nature of the stimulus situation.

The nature of the stimulus-response relationship in gestalt theory is theologically valid. As a scientific theory it cannot speak of responses to revelation, but its understanding of responses does not require revelation to be an unacceptable factor just because it resists objective analysis. Revelation insists that God communicates himself in his free movement to man and his reception by man. The stimulus is directed to the human cognitive faculty, and man as a self-determining agent exercises his responsible option to respond in a particular way. This approach to the stimulus-response relationship is congenial with gestalt theory.

*The learner is an intelligent self-active being who is to be comprehended by observation of his behavior in relationship and through his internal frame of reference.*

Gestalt experiments began with studies in perception. This origin is reflected in the definition of the learner. He is viewed in terms of behavior consonant with his capacity for perceiving relationships. In gestalt experiments, elements for the solution are always present. These need to be combined in a new way. How the problem is solved indicates intelligence rather than blind searching. The self concept is acknowledged as necessary for any theory that seeks to explain human learning. It is possible to know something of man by listening to how he feels about a situation. His perceptions are necessary sources for self-knowledge. This does not exclude the validity of the observer's notes if these are not absolutized.

Gestalt theory's view of the learner is theologically valid. According to the doctrine of man, man is a creature related to lower creatures. But unlike them, he is a self capable of transcendence, determination, and of restructuring his field of relationships before overt responding. He is a responsible being. All of these characteristics of man have been articulated by representatives of gestalt theory at one point or another. Therefore, there is nothing invalid about the gestalt approach to the learner. Theology, however, must present its distinctive insights. In the final analysis, man is known only in relationship with God.

*The context of learning is the physical field beyond the learner, the psychological field within, and the tension which holds them in relationship.*

Physical field means the visible external situation such as objects, events, persons, problems, and words. By psychological field is meant the learner and his perception of the physical field. An object may be physically distant and yet be psychologically near because it is now present in either the visual or memory field. The tension system as part of the context indicates that the line of stimulation is not from without " in," but that the field of force moves in two directions. The learner is both acted upon by the stimuli and in turn acts upon them. If the context is under the control of anyone, it is the learner. Admittedly, the educator may and must give guidance in structuring the problem, but all elements for the solution must be present. In gestalt, the educator does not exercise a totalitarian function to bring about the correct response. In this sense, the context is open and free.

Theologically, the context of learning is the church. Persons learn as they participate in the life and the mission of the church. There is opportunity for mutual address and response through the quality of interpersonal relations. A " spirit " is present in the group which facilitates learning and hinders it if absent. These essential elements are not challenged by gestalt theory's concept of the context of learning. Gestalt theory is considered theologically valid although it needs to be supplemented by the church's own self-interpretation.

*Learning occurs because of the dynamics of tension induced in the learner by the unresolved character of the goal, and by the reorganization of the perceived field as a cognitive act.*

Tension is present as a force between the goal-object and the learner. But unlike that in reinforcement theory, drop in tension does not cause repetition of behavior. This is evident in insight experiments where understanding of the solution always precedes its execution. Therefore, tension induction rather than reduction is an effective dynamic for gestalt theory.

By persisting at a problem, the learner utilizes past experiences, but they are structured in a new manner. Until the learner perceives the essential relationships of the problem, it remains insoluble. When the problem has been learned and is again presented, the perceived field is readily reorganized as a cognitive decision. This often occurs suddenly and without the searching movements characteristic of trial-and-error learning. Unlike conditioning, the dynamics of gestalt theory operate through the central rather than the peripheral nervous system. The muscle cells are effectors of responses determined by the intelligent decision of the learner rather than co-ordinators. In all learning, the basic motive power is the choice of perceptions that enhance the self. The tension already described occurs because the unresolved character of the goal is perceived as a threat to the self until realized. If the problem to be learned is of no concern to the self, no amount of coercion will attain learning that persists.

The suddenness characteristic of the action of the Holy

Spirit finds a reference point in gestalt theory. The theorists need not accept the operation of the Holy Spirit. Their theoretical formulations permit a certain " openness " in the process of learning. Intuitive as well as analytical procedures have integrity. During the course of study with a particular learning task, the learner often arrives at the answer in a dramatic way. He " sees " the essential relationships in a moment of time. All the factors were there at the beginning of the task, but not until they were cognitively rearranged could the elements become the correct whole. It is apparent that the Holy Spirit works in similar ways. Persons may study the Bible and worship with the congregation without any visible change in attitudes, values, or motives. Then at a certain hour, the entire relationship is perceived in a way that has ultimate significance for the self. In the language of theology, the Holy Spirit has effected a transformation; he has guided the individual to a deeper level of learning. Because gestalt theory provides for free and intelligent responses, its dynamic has theological integrity. It nonetheless requires the specification of the Holy Spirit as the power for Christian nurture for its dynamic to be wholly valid.

4. *Sign-Gestalt Theory and Theology*

*Responses are cognitions of the learner.*

According to sign-gestalt theory, stimuli do not have an autonomous function of evoking reflex-type responses. Stimuli become material for the learner's perceptual faculties. Stated in another way, a response is not an act that is done; it is knowledge that determines what to do.

Sign-gestalt theory's view of responses as cognitions is congruent with a theological interpretation. Responses in revelation are cognitive in nature. God becomes known and man perceives himself in a new way. The continuing revelation may issue in responses that are more than knowledge, but they cannot be less. Since sign-gestalt theory affirms responses that permit a relationship with God's self-disclosure to man, its approach to the recurrence of responses is theologically acceptable.

*The learner is a purposive being described in cognitive terms from a behavioristic orientation.*

No distinction is made among various orders of learners. Principles derived from studies of lower animals may be generalized to include man.

Were the words, " from a behavioristic orientation " not included in the definition of the learner, sign-gestalt's position on the learner would be theologically valid. The cognitive terminology such as, " purposes," " expectations," " signs," " significates," " perceptions," and " inferences " all indicate that theology could be in fruitful dialogue with sign-gestalt theory. These are words which theology could use without apology to describe man. As a covenant partner of God, man is both responsible and purposive. He has a destiny beyond the present space-time but seeks to express God's purpose for him in this space-time. Man uses verbal signs and symbols to define central concerns of the covenant community. He perceives relationships, obtains meanings, and draws inferences for novel situations. But are the theological meanings considered agreeable with cognitive terminology accurate? This is the problem which sign-gestalt theory raises for theological validation.

Theology must determine whether it will reach an evaluative judgment of sign-gestalt theory in terms of its expression or its intent. If other theorists were certain that sign-gestalt theory is in fact behavioristic, the decision would be simplified. Some behavioristic theorists are inclined to consider sign-learning a nonobjective mentalism. Were this the case, theology could then feel confident in evaluating sign-gestalt theory's view of the learner as compatible with the Christian doctrine of man. This procedure, although attractive, is inaccurate.

Sign-gestalt theory is intended to be a behaviorism. The raw data are the observable events. The learner as purposeful is meant to imply no more than the experimenter's note that a learner's behavior is oriented in a forward direction. It is seeking to reach a goal. Expectations are descriptions of the learner's apparent anticipation of a goal-object, but this is from the observer's point of view. If sign-gestalt theory intends to be behavioristic, then it is not clear that so-called purposive behavior is really different from trial-and-error learning. Should this be the case, sign-gestalt theory's view of the learner would be theologically invalid. For the doctrine of man, purposive responses are less the inferences of an observer and more the choices appropriate to the intellectual capacity of the learner. Purpose is the decision of a responsible self.

To the degree that sign-gestalt theory is a behaviorism, it is theologically invalid in its description of the learner. As a behaviorism, there is no place for a transcendent self. However, if its terminology stands for more than behavioristic events, if its key words are taken seriously, sign-gestalt theory is theologically valid.

*The context of learning is a gestalt-whole formed by the learner, the goal, the sign, and the process to the goal.*

It is affirmed that the place of learning is complex. The environment does not act on the learner at the instigation of the educator as in conditioning. Neither is the environment merely an enclosure in which the learner is free to find a solution. The environment provides for mutual interaction. It includes the needs of the learner, the attractiveness of the goal, and the cues that the learner uses to find its way to the goal-solution.

There is nothing indicated here which negates the essential nature of the church as the place where learning occurs in Christian nurture. The learner in the church is a member of the body of Christ rather than an isolated being. Through the quality of the church's life and the power of the Holy Spirit, the church acts on the learner even as the learner addresses the church. This is an interpersonal exchange. The church provides certain signs through worship, the Bible, and theology which become the content of learning. All these elements form a whole which is greater than the sum of the parts. In the context of wholeness, the learner opens himself to basic learning because man needs to be part of a healthy social structure.

*The dynamics of learning are seen as functions of the relationships discerned between two or more physical or psychophysical events.*

Where the learner perceives that a course of action results in the achievement of a goal, on subsequent occasions a similar procedure will be expected to realize the goal. Knowledge is achieved. Even though the goal may not be physically present, through developed cognitions it is psychologically present. Instead of engaging in trial-and-error behavior, the learner utilizes its knowledge of what leads to what. Each apparently wrong action is not an instance of stupid behavior but an unconfirmed hypothesis that had been submitted for testing. Unconfirmed hypotheses are rejected while those confirmed are repeated. Learners are held to their tasks of perceiving relationships and of testing hypotheses through the valence of the goal-object, that is, its attractiveness for the learner.

As learners in the church perceive relationships between themselves and the whole field of relationships, including God, dependable knowledge is gained. Where specific decisions do not fulfill anticipations either of the individual or the covenant community, they are intentionally discontinued. By describing motivation as the valence of the goal-object, sign-gestalt theory avoids the pitfalls of reinforcement theory. A goal may be attractive in a larger context even though there is no reinforcement, properly speaking. This appears to be the case when Christians seek to live as disciples in a hostile world.

Although sign-gestalt theory is an avowed behaviorism, its description of the dynamics of learning is relatively unstructured. The lack of precision in the theory permits the inclusion of the Holy Spirit as either a valence or as a field force resulting in a reorganization of relationships as perceived. Because the dynamics take account of the perspective of the learner and the field organization of the context, the latter may be considered theologically acceptable.

All the theories' insights into the four concerns judged of worth to both theology and learning theory possess theological validity to varying degrees. The behavioristic approaches cause more theological problems than those which are less rigid. More questions are raised by theology about the learner in learning and the dynamics of learning as these are answered by learning theory than other concerns. These two areas are critical for the development of a learning theory for Christian nurture which has theological validity as well as functional adequacy.

## Learning Theory, Theology, and the Concerns to Be Learned

It is now possible to pick up the concerns to be learned in Christian nurture in order to check the theological integrity and functional adequacy of each theory's answers to the seven concerns. As has been indicated,[8] a representative learning problem is selected for each concern and a concise statement offered for the respective learning theory's solution to it. The learning theory answer will be evaluated theologically.

### 1. *Reinforcement Theory and the Concerns to Be Learned*

*Knowledge* of the mighty acts of God in Israel's history is a function of searching behavior and of the reward for the correct response or the nonreward for the incorrect response. On future occasions when the stimulus inquiry is presented for the mighty acts of God, response answers previously rewarded will tend to be repeated. Those not rewarded will be disregarded.

The acquisition of knowledge-facts in reinforcement theory has theological integrity because God's revelation does not come apart from an awareness of the Biblical witness. To acquire knowledge of how God has acted is usually the precursor to genuine encounter with God. The problem of knowledge learning is less how it is attained and more whether the theoretical approach results in a reservoir of factual material. Reinforcement theory's evidence indicates that knowledge responses do occur.

Hypotheses have been presented by reinforcement theorists to explain *understanding*. But these do not offer a reliable basis for predicting how Biblical knowledge fragments may be brought together for the whole of understanding the Bible as the drama of redemption. Accordingly, no validation may be undertaken except to observe that Christian nurture must look elsewhere for insight into the process of learning that issues in growth in understanding.

Learning the *attitude* of *agapē* love occurs through searching behavior in a social context under reinforcement. The learner consciously or unconsciously tries out behavioral action to see what kinds of responses are elicited from other persons. If the responses are accepted as satisfying to the learner, they will be repeated and consequently learned.

Attitudes are learned and unlearned through reinforcement, but the question remains whether reinforcement theory is either theologically valid or pragmatically effective for all of the human attitudes desired in Christian nurture. Persons should learn to participate in the world of persons with the attitude of love. Were the proper reinforcement discovered, love would follow as a necessary consequence. However, if human sin is as serious a factor as is portrayed in the doctrine of man, then no amount of reward will change the most deep-seated attitudes. Learning to love in the theological conception of process is directly related to an acknowledged encounter with God issuing in redemption. The encounter may come as the Holy Spirit mediates Biblical knowledge in a particular situation of abiding concern. The encounter may be experienced in the community of the church since it is a redemptive organism. Whatever may be the specifics of the relationship, it is the means for effecting a change in the attitude of persons.

For the more general attitudes, such as fair play, honesty, and the like, reinforcement theory may be theologically valid. The emphasis is upon *may*. Reinforcement may be adequate until the attitude is met by a formidable challenge that releases suspicions and antagonisms. Now the attitude learned under reinforcement may be inadequate. Instead of reinforcement, there is required the dynamic of the Holy Spirit. Therefore, reinforcement theory is deficient because reward is held to do a work that can be accomplished by the Holy Spirit alone.

The church as *value* is learned to the degree that personal need states are satisfied. It is not presumed that trial-and-error experiences are undertaken only under guidance of the church. For the church to be considered as value, there are likely to be searching experiences with other structures in society. If the church is found to be more personally satisfying than other organizations, it will be valued.

There is no disputing that value is learned under reinforcement. There is theological validity in this affirmation. In the doctrine of man, personal identity is learned in relationship and through the quality of those relationships. The potential for relationships of worth in the church is at a maximum since the church is a redemptive organism. Unless human needs appropriate to the church are met, the church is neither true to its nature nor to its purpose. To the degree that the church is identified as significant because of its functions, reinforcement theory's answer to value is valid.

However, there is more to a theological view of value.

Theology conceives of the church as value because of what it is as well as what it may do. To reduce the church as value to a hedonistic level violates the purpose of God implied in the church as a covenant community. It has value for witness irrespective of whether or not experiences in it are personally rewarding.

The absence of any conception of the learner as transcendent causes reinforcement theory to be further invalid and inadequate for value learning in Christian nurture. Value is related to a self-determining person. Value is also an emotional response of the self in encounter with God. If the self is not specified in reinforcement theory, the latter cannot be a valid explanation for value learning.

The *skill* of worship is learned through an investigation of various forms and traditions of worship. Experiences that are satisfying will be repeated. As more of the unrewarded responses drop out, a particular worship pattern becomes both a skill and a habit. If leading in worship is a variation of the skill to be learned, the same general principles hold true. The style of leadership tends to be a reflection of the occasions when certain procedures reduced threats, tensions, and as a consequence gave the leader a sense of command of the situation.

As members of the creaturely order, persons strive for general equilibrium. Tensions may be alleviated and successful operations repeated. To the extent that worship is the learning of satisfying patterns and mechanics, reinforcement theory is theologically valid for the skill-habit learning.

Where worship goes beyond rewarding patterns of action, reinforcement theory is invalid. In worship, person-to-person encounter is central. The meeting may be satisfying, but this is not its critical characteristic. In worship there is disclosure and response, summons and acceptance. Furthermore, if the accent is upon reward there may be a tendency to overlook the corporate character of worship. What is good for the individual takes precedence over an acknowledged relationship with the church as the body of Christ. No learning theory is valid if the organismic character of the church is neglected. This does not mean that reinforcement theory is supposed to have a theory of the church. But it does mean that the theoretical structure must not stress individualism to the prejudice of the corporate life.

*Motive* learning is a minor concern in reinforcement theory because motives are the basis for learning. The organism is stimulated to take such action as will reduce a particular drive. Other drives may be learned if rewarded, but learned drives are not helpful for such motives as discipleship. Were the hedonistic law of effect expanded to include some kind of reward involved in losing one's life for the sake of Christ, the basic identity of reinforcement would be lost and would, therefore, become meaningless. The more responsible procedure appears to be to acknowledge that reinforcement theory is both invalid and inadequate for the motives peculiar to Christian nurture. Discipleship of Christ is a motive that leads to service of God rather than to a necessary satisfaction of the person.

Since reinforcement theory attempts to explain all learning at the animal level, there is no provision for descriptions of *change in the self*. Even though there is no provision for the self, the latter may be changed as part of reinforcement learning, but this has no necessary part of the theory. Accordingly, there is no basis for validation.

### 2. *Conditioning Theory and the Concerns to Be Learned*

*Knowledge* of the mighty acts of God in Israel's history is learned through the teacher's structuring of the stimulus situation in such a way that when the stimulus is presented of God acting in history, the appropriate knowledge response will be given. Particular attention is devoted to muscular movements of the learner as conditioners for responses. Doing is related to knowing.

Man is more than a reactive creature, but he is reactive. Because this is true, the heritage of the community may be communicated through verbal symbols. Generally consistent response patterns elicited by verbal symbols constitute knowledge in the psychological sense. Such an appraisal is in agreement with man as a creature. Man is a sinner, but he is capable of acquiring knowledge consistent with his creaturely status. This means that the conditioning paradigm is valid for learning about God's actions in behalf of Israel.

It would not be correct to assume that knowledge gained elsewhere than by conditioning is less than knowledge. Genuine knowledge is also the result of revelation. In relation to God, man comes to receive knowledge of God rather than about him and knowledge of the self rather than about the self. Neither knowledge of God nor of the self is the result of movement-produced stimuli or substitute cues. Where conditioning, then, is considered true for all learning, it is invalid.

*Understanding* the Bible as the drama of redemption is a conditioned response and as much a matter of habit as any physical skill. Conditioning explains the acquisitions of knowledge, but its approach to understanding fails to be convincing.

Theology is not ready to solve the problem so easily. In conditioning, the role of the " understander " in relating parts and wholes is ignored. He is part of a habit system. Yet man as a responsible learner is the antithesis of a habit organism. There is no responsibility if responses are habitual. However, if man is a responsible learner, then he is held accountable for what he understands. To be held accountable implies the active participation of a person in relating parts and wholes. Since such a one is absent in conditioning theory, it must be theologically invalid for understandings in Christian nurture.

The *attitude* of *agapē* love is learned through the correlation of the stimulus of love-as-a-person and the love response of the learner. According to conditioning postulates, love is learned on the one occurrence of the stimulus and the response. Because there are so many situations in which the attitude of love should be expressed, however, the learning of love is a long-time process under many circumstances. Originally, love is a response to a loving person. Later, the concept of love may evoke the action of love. There has been conditioning. But the attitude of love has been learned within a limited dimension. Ultimately, the attitude must be so learned that it persists even when the substitute stimuli of anger, hate, and indifference are presented.

Conditioning's approach to attitudinal change is commendable from the perspective of the doctrine of man if other persons are identified as the stimuli. If man learns in relationship, then attention needs to be given to the quality of the relationships that become stimuli for other persons. When learners in the church are stimulated by other persons, the response of love follows quite naturally. But what happens when the substitute stimuli are not loving persons? How does love become the response attitude to the stimuli of pain? Conditioning's conception of attitudinal learning would indicate that love could not be the response if the stimuli were not conducive to it.

Where the attitude to be learned is a response of steadfast concern for another's well-being regardless of circumstances, conditioning is invalid. It would presume to predict all attitudinal learning within a natural process. Rather than an attitude that must follow if the manipulative conditions can be specified, love is a response learned through the work of the Holy Spirit. Man as a sinner needs a basic change in himself if he is to love. *Agapē* love is an emotional and volitional response to God rather than to conditioned stimuli.

The church as *value* is learned as responses are elicited that involve the learner in the life of the church. Stimuli of the church taking itself seriously have a tendency to evoke responses of a serious attitude toward it. Now the substitute stimulus of the word " church " may result in the same value relationship as the church as experienced.

Value learning in conditioning is valid within the frame of reference described. However, it is doubtful whether conditioning theory's answer to value learning is theologically acceptable because of its premise that the learner is continuous with nature. Lower organisms may have an attraction for certain objects, but this is not the same as the value concern of a self-conscious person. Value is more than a conditioned response; it is a positive cathexis for an object determined worthy of attention. Such a process requires the existence of a self. Since for conditioning theory, the self is no necessary category, it cannot be valid for value learning in Christian nurture.

The *skill* of worship is learned through the responses made by the learner to the stimulus situation. Each skill is a collection of habits. The muscle movements involved in worship become the conditioners for future actions where similar external stimuli are present. Guidance in the skill of worship must anticipate what the initial response patterns will be. Neither instruction nor action will result in desired learning if these occur when the learner is engaged in other activity. Verbal comments then become signs for continued disinterest. If the stimulus situation causes the learner to be attentive and to participate in the worship experience, however, he will learn to be attentive and willing to share in worship. Furthermore, the skill of worship will be facilitated if the stimulus situation for learning is also the context for actual worship.

To the extent that worship is a muscular exercise, the theory of conditioning is necessary and valid. The worshipers are not disembodied spirits. They are bodies. But as with all skills in the church's life, doing does not become a substitute for understanding. Doing is one of the factors, and admittedly, an important one.

Yet worship is more than action. In worship, the church

is expressing the nature that God has imputed to it. It is giving thanks for the greatness of his redemption. Since conditioning is handicapped in dealing with worship as more than muscular action, it lacks complete validity for the skill-habit learning of Christian nurture.

*Motives* do not appear to be learned in conditioning. They are already present in the situation. Their significance is not directly necessary for learning. Motives cause the learner to do something. What is done is learned rather than the motive. Motivation, such as to the life of discipleship, is beyond the conditioning paradigm and consequently, conditioning must be evaluated as functionally inadequate, and theologically invalid.

As with reinforcement theory, conditioning is without authority to account for *change in the self*. No self concept is acknowledged. Therefore, conditioning is invalid for the change in the self through Christian nurture.

3. *Gestalt Theory and Concerns to Be Learned*

*Knowledge* of the mighty acts of God in Israel's history is a response to Biblical relationships. Gestalt theory does not speak of knowledge resulting from responses to presented stimuli. Knowledge is gained obliquely. As the learner relates parts and wholes, he is acquiring knowledge of the parts. These parts have meaning in relationship with other facts learned from the Bible rather than as individual entities.

The gestalt approach to knowledge of the mighty acts of God is theologically valid. In revelation, the event and revelatory situation belong together. By the learner's relating potential knowledge fragments with the circumstances of the moment, more reliable information is gained. The learner is actively participating in the acquisition of knowledge. This position is also congenial with the doctrine of man as a responsible being.

Gestalt theory's reliance upon knowledge through tension systems in the field of relationships provides sufficient flexibility to include the operation of the Holy Spirit. It also issues in knowledge learning.

*Understanding* the Bible as the drama of redemption is a function of the learner's object field and the consequent psychophysical tension system. Elements of the object field must be physically or psychologically present. This means that factors necessary for understanding must be within the intellectual and chronological capacity of the learner as well as his educational development. Once the elements are present, the learner is motivated by an inner tension to find a solution to the presented problem. Parts may be related to one another and insight achieved.

Once understanding has been achieved, it tends to persist as a permanent learning. When the occasion demands, the Bible as the drama of redemption is defined without the careful field organization necessary for the initial learning experiences. The understanding gained now becomes another part of the learner's complex field of relationships to be utilized in future novel situations for the life of faith.

Gestalt's view of understanding is validated by the doctrines of man and the Holy Spirit. The gestalt man is intelligent, active, and purposeful. He gives evidence of being a responsible learner. As the person is taught by the Holy Spirit, he comes to new understandings never anticipated previously. Since insight bearing a relationship with the action of the Holy Spirit is in operation for gestalt theory, the latter is theologically valid for its learning to understand the Bible as the drama of redemption.

The *attitude* of *agapē* love is a product of the learner's field of relationships. If there are no elements of love in the field, the attitude learning of love is impossible.

Love is learned through love experiences in the learner's field of relationships such as persons, the community of the church, and the larger society of the world. If the learner finds himself to be the object of disrespect or prejudice, the elements of prejudice and love may be restructured to show the error of prejudice and the necessity of love.

Love in the doctrine of man is the answering of the whole man. It is man's cognitive, volitional, and emotional response to God. In the gestalt approach, attitudinal change is probably more cognitive than anything else. This does not exclude the emotions, but neither are they necessarily included. If the attitude is to be changed, guidance must be given to help the learner perceive his field from a different perspective. This is the procedure of psychotherapy. In so far as the learner may modify his relationships perceptually, gestalt theory is adequate.

However, attitudes are affected by sin. Hence they cannot be changed by human effort alone. If love is learned in the *agapē* form, it must be through the redemptive working of God in the church by the Holy Spirit. Without the Holy Spirit as the active power restructuring man's way of perceiving the field of relationships, gestalt theory's interpretation for learning the attitude of love is invalid.

The church as *value* is a function of the learner's need for the church's life and the distinctiveness of the church in the learner's perceived field. Both aspects are significant. The learner must have a sense of need before the church can be valued. What the need is affects the degree of value. If the need is for altruistic service, the church may have value at this level. Furthermore, there must be something sufficiently distinctive about the church for it to stand out from among other possible institutions. As the learner finds his needs met, the church as value will be learned.

Gestalt theory's conception of value acquisition is theologically valid because it posits an active, responsible learner being modified by the quality of his relationships. A responsible learner may have a positive cathexis for value at a level that is beyond the reactive man. However, once the structural validity is acknowledged, there is no appreciable advance in gestalt theory. It lacks theological and functional adequacy because the critical norm is absent. If value is the product of need, then how the need is specified becomes the significant issue. For the church to be valued, it must guide the learner to at least a cognitive apprehension of man as sinner. Once man's lost condition is perceived, the church's message and life of redemption may meet the learner's basic need. At the same time, the learner's field of relationships must include the church. How this organization stands out from other social structures as the answer to his need determines how it is valued.

The *skill* of worship is learned through a consideration of the broad patterns of worship first of all, and then through attention to such specifics as barriers to worship, resources, and physical movements.

Because theology emphasizes that man comes to know himself, other persons, and God, in relationship, gestalt theory's view of skill-habit learning is valid. Reinforcement and conditioning theories are helpful for explaining the gaining of techniques of worship, but they fall short of its justification. In gestalt theory, movement and meaning may be held together. Knowing the place of the parts in the whole and that the whole is more than the parts, the learner gains insight into the skill habits of worship. He understands why Scripture is followed by responses of prayer and hymn, for example. He comprehends why worship is expressed differently in various traditions. There is learning as part of this total relationship.

The *motive* of discipleship is learned as the learner identifies the nature of the gospel and the opportunities for Christian witness as existing in his psychophysical field. When these elements become perceived as significant to the self, the foundation is established for learning the life of the disciple.

As a structural description of motive learning, gestalt theory is valid. The doctrine of the church holds out possibilities for basic learning as learners share in the life of the covenant community. Here God is able to break through to guide changes in the individual, including his motives. However, changed motives are more than cognitive acts. Motives in Christian nurture are responses to God's disclosure in Jesus Christ. This is a necessary qualifying factor for a theological validation of gestalt theory in motive learning.

*Change in the self* is the result of changes in cognitive structure, understandings, attitudes, values, and motives. However, the gestalt model has no necessary formulations for the radical changes in the self anticipated through relationship with God. Christian nurture conceives of changes resulting in a point of view requiring a deep personal commitment to Jesus Christ. Gestalt theory may take the learner to the discovery of meaning, but it must stop short of the self responding to God's disclosure. It does, it will be remembered, have a place for the self, however. This permits it to be more adequate than the other theories investigated, but it falls short of theological validity.

4. *Sign-Gestalt Theory and the Concerns to Be Learned*

*Knowledge* of the mighty acts of God in Israel's history is attained through giving attention to the criteria that eventually become identified as "mighty acts." The responses made to the components of God's acting in history are maintained as cognitions. Knowledge-facts gained are not in isolation. They are discerned as necessary means to the goal-object of the mighty acts of God.

According to theology, revelation is for man. This implies he is able to perceive the revelation. He is an active, intelligent being capable of grasping segments of knowledge for purposeful decisions. Since this is not contradicted by the sign-gestalt hypothesis, the theory may be considered theologically valid in so far as knowledge is a natural relationship.

*Understanding* the Bible as the drama of redemption is learned as a response to a field of relationships, such as Biblical facts and the testimony of Christian experience. Knowledge facts of the Bible gained on previous occasions are present in memory. In other areas of the Christian life, the learner has had experience in perceptual responses. He has examined data and drawn conclusions from them. Inferences have been utilized for other novel situations. Now all of these, memory, perception, and inferences are joined together to develop understanding, or in the terminology of the theory, a new sign-gestalt of understanding. Instead of the extra effort of trial-and-error learning, sign-gestalt theory stresses that the learner acts on the basis of meanings gained. These are used to solve problems purposefully.

As with knowledge acquisition, sign-gestalt theory represents a position that corresponds with the intelligent learner evident in revelation and the Christian view of man. On this basis, sign-gestalt theory's approach to understanding-learning is theologically valid.

The *attitude* of *agapē* love is learned as a product of the learner's perception of a segment in his interpersonal field of relationships. If the learner perceives his relationships as personally enriching, he will develop at the least an attitude of well-being. Should the segment of the field issue in a traumatic experience, the attitude will be negative. On future occasions, there will be the expectation of trauma. If this is confirmed, the attitude of avoidance will be learned rather than love.

With its concern about relationships as the principal factor for attitude learning, sign-gestalt theory is theologically valid. The doctrines of man and the church bear witness to the truth that relationships are significant for depth in learning. However, the approach is valid only in the initial phases of Christian nurture. Ultimately, Christian nurture desires that the attitude of *agapē* love be learned with less dependence upon personal satisfaction. Love as concern for the other must not be limited by expectations that love will be received. Instead of the confirmation of this hope, love requires steadfastness even when the person's outgoing attitude receives hate and rejection. Therefore, sign-gestalt theory is also invalid for certain aspects of attitudinal learning.

*Value* is understood in sign-gestalt theory as the object or substance to be approached or avoided by the learner in a given need state. The church as value then is learned to the degree the learner's expectancies of the moment are confirmed. If the church is anticipated as the place where koinonia is known, and experience confirms this to be true, the church will have value. However, if the church is anticipated as a kind of service club and experience indicates that this is not true, the particular church will not be valued.

At a superficial level, sign-gestalt theory's position on value learning is valid. The church cannot expect to be valued if in it persons do not find their deepest needs realized. As a redemptive organism, the church teaches value by what it is. Value learning, however, that is wholly dependent upon need lacks the ability to account for value as deemed essential in Christian nurture. If the doctrine of the church is true, then the church has value in virtue of God's decision to be present with it in power. Value must be learned that perceives the church as significant as an act of responsible faith. Furthermore, value in Christian nurture is the positive decision of the self. Since the self is not a category in sign-gestalt theory, the analysis of value learning falls short of the norm and is lacking in theological validity.

The *skill* of worship is learned as the learner takes cognizance of such cues as movements, feelings, the devotional treasury of the church, and the meaning of worship. Skill is the discovery of purposeful relationships. Through practice, expressions of worship come into closer harmony with anticipations of what the church understands it to be. This is not to say that practice alone is sufficient. The critical factor is the " feedback " from the various signs established by the church. As the learner interprets these signs, he makes adjustments in his expression of worship.

Christian theology's emphasis upon responsibility in the individual and the corporate life validates sign-gestalt theory's description of skill learning. Meaning and movement are both adequately related. Yet it is possible that cognition may carry more than is theologically advisable. Worship involves all the elements described, but it is primarily a response to God. This is beyond the theoretical capacity of sign-gestalt theory.

*Motives* are learned as functions of the meaning of the goal route and the confirmation of expectancies in practice. If the learner is to make decisions under the motivation of discipleship, he must develop cognitions about its requirements. Should the intended venture of discipleship indicate a confirmation of what was anticipated, discipleship as a motive may become learned as part of the sign-gestalt of the Christian life, that is, the total expression of Christian faith and life. If expectations are unconfirmed, if there was a greater cost in discipleship than anticipated, according to the theory, discipleship as a motive should not be learned.

As with value learning, discipleship as a motive may be theologically valid at superficial levels and yet be invalid for Christian nurture. Man as God's covenant partner is called to unconditional responsibility. Discipleship is thus learned as a response to God's initiative. Because of this element of personal response and commitment, sign-gestalt theory is largely invalid for motive learning in Christian nurture.

Since sign-gestalt theory is an admitted behaviorism, there is no provision for the self and as a consequence, no anticipation of *change in the self*. There is only a purposeful learner who is intent upon realizing ends in an intelligent manner. Whether man is accepted as a self or not, he remains one. As he acts upon the environment of the moment, he is also changed. He is partially a product of his organized perceptions. Therefore when he is engaged in learning tasks according to the sign-gestalt paradigm, he is doubtlessly being changed. But this is in spite of the theory rather than because of it. Because the self is not a part of the structure of sign-gestalt thinking, Christian nurture must look elsewhere for insights in the kind of changes anticipated where the self is in relationship to God.

No one theory is either functionally adequate or theologically valid for all of the concerns to be learned in Christian nurture. Each is able to provide foundations for learning tasks that have the possibility of issuing in general growth. Gestalt theory offers the best hope for a single theory. But it, too, is deficient particularly at the place where Christian nurture is more than a horizontal experience. Christian nurture requires God's initiative in the totality of learning. No theory has this critical factor.

## Chapter VI

# An Outline of a Theory

BEFORE a suggested theory of learning for Christian nurture is outlined, a brief résumé of the thought thus far may prove useful. The study began with a survey of the problem of learning as viewed from the perspective of representative Christian education theorists. On the basis of research to date, it was apparent that the relationship between learning theory and theology for Christian education purposes needed further exploration. To specify the questions which required answers by any theory of learning with pretensions for adequacy, expositions were offered of seven concerns to be learned in Christian nurture. Next, four representative theories of learning were studied, according to their basic paradigms and in terms of their strengths and weaknesses. At this point, learning theory was set aside for the time being in order to express the theological foundations for process and evaluation. Finally, the disciplines of learning theory and theology were brought into an evaluative relationship through an analysis of issues common to them. The greatest problems for learning theory as theory were in the areas of the learner and the dynamics of learning. Further evaluations were made of each theory's probable response to each of the seven concerns to be learned in Christian nurture. Gestalt theory was the one approach with the greatest general integrity, but it suffered with the others from an inability to encompass the divine frame of reference in learning.

Certain questions now need to be answered. What are

the necessary minimum data for a theory from learning theory and theology? Can these be restructured to issue in a new theory of learning? Is the new theory functionally adequate and theologically valid to meet the concerns to be learned in Christian nurture?

The proposed theory of learning must draw upon the factual evidences for learning without being committed to the particular form in which these facts have been used for the building of theory in the past. This is a procedure held in respect among learning theorists themselves. No learning theorist denies the facts of other experimenters. The facts are reinterpreted either to corroborate the theory espoused or to indicate that the preferred theory is not contradicted by the new experimental data.

Certain fundamental facts have been discovered through the investigations of learning theorists:

Learning is dependent upon the physical, psychological, and intellectual need states of the learner. In learning theory parlance, this is usually described as " readiness."

Learners frequently engage in searching behavior prior to reaching the goal-solution and consequently, the achievement of learning.

Action patterns that resulted in a satisfying state of affairs for the learner tend to be repeated when similar conditions are present which called forth the original action. Patterns that issued in an unsatisfactory state of affairs tend to be dropped. The factors of reward and non-reward, however, are modified by evidence for growth motivation and the perceptual involvement of the self.

Muscle movements as responses may become conditioners for further responses. The kinesthetic sensations are both co-ordinators and confirmers of learning. A learner's actions are indicators of what has been learned.

Insight is a manifestation of intelligent problem-solving by perceiving organisms without going through the process of searching behavior. Learners may respond to, and consequently learn through, relationships.

Learning occurs through tension systems activated in the learner through his concern for self-integrity, the character of the goal-object, and the context as a whole. The learner receives impressions or feedback from the entire experience, which are then reorganized.

The self concept is a necessity for expressing human behavior. How the individual perceives himself and his relationship to the not-self world affects what is learned.

Even as there are basic facts from learning theory, so there are also theological insights which need articulation:

Revelation is the divine act of disclosure to man in Jesus Christ. It occurs as the mutual address and response of dialogue with deep involvement in the Biblical witness. Revelation is the fact plus its reception by perceiving selves. Furthermore, in revelation, the event and the revelatory situation belong together. This means that the church is the primary locus of revelation.

As God's covenant partner, man is a responsible learner coming to the deepest learning in relationship. He is self-conscious and self-transcendent with a divine destiny. Although he has this singular identity, he is also a sinner. This means that man cannot restructure his field of relationships to fulfill their proper purposes. His perceptual processes are included in his alienation from God. If man is to learn and to come into his full humanity, he must be empowered by the Holy Spirit.

The church is the covenant community, the body of Christ, the fellowship of the Holy Spirit. These terms indicate that God's resources are present in the church for the totality of its life, including its nurture. Growth is, therefore, more than a natural process. It is the result of God's fashioning a people. Even though the church is God's decision for the context of Christian nurture, it may respond in faith or disobedience. Whether faithful or unfaithful, the church communicates its faith through the nature of its life.

The Holy Spirit is the "remembrancer," the one who

causes fruit to be borne in the learner's life, the developer of koinonia in the church. He guides the perceptual processes of man so that these may issue in the most fundamental level of learning — change in the self. As the dynamic of learning, the Spirit is not bound by closed systems. He works with them but is beyond them.

## The Theory Defined

The problem to be faced in the development of a learning theory for Christian nurture is the organization of existing data from theology and learning theory in such a way that their critical insights are preserved. The theory must be sufficiently exclusive to avoid connotations of theories evaluated as theologically deficient, and yet be inclusive enough to encompass the necessary conclusions gained from laboratory research.

Since only gestalt theory approximates all of the concerns to be learned in Christian nurture, it is conceivable that a modified gestalt theory could be adequate. It has not made all of the learning-theory evidence central to its expression, but none of the valid psychological material is denied. When it comes to a handling of the theological data, the adequacy of gestalt theory is less convincing. Theological insights are foreign to the theory although the field of relationships can be expanded to include the church and the Holy Spirit. But to use gestalt theory in this manner is to violate its integrity. It is a matter of appropriation without specifying the range of applicability of the theory. There is nothing intrinsically theological about gestalt formulations. Theological sources would need to be drawn in from the outside to serve a qualifying function. Accordingly, gestalt theory even though modified must be rejected as the basic theory of learning for Christian nurture.[1]

Another theory which has much to commend itself is that of " learning by encounter." It could be the means to integrate the theological and psychological insights. But the problem is in the ambiguity of its terminology. There is no way of knowing whether the major frame of reference will be theological or psychological. If the encounter takes its stance from a theological orientation, there is a place for the free operation of the Holy Spirit. Through the encounter with God's revelation in Jesus Christ, the learner may respond in faith and love. Learning can be a personal decision affecting the most existential action processes of the learner. Were a theory of this type anticipated as supplementary in character, it would be adequate for Christian nurture. If it were intended to bring the theological and the learning-theory insights into relationship, its weaknesses are obvious. On the other hand, if encounter is perceived in its psychological dimensions, the necessary theological concerns are likely to be overlooked. Encounter with God may be part of the whole cluster of relationships which issue in learning, but the action of God is not postulated as an imperative. Therefore, because a learning theory of encounter lacks precision, the need is not met for an inclusive theory of learning for Christian nurture.

A different proposal could be a frank combination of the psychological with the theological such as "ego-involvement under guidance of the Holy Spirit." It is very close to what is needed. The person's active participation in learning is preserved. At the same time, ego learning is considered as limited. There must be guidance by the Holy Spirit. How the learner perceives his field of relationships and his role in those relationships is dependent upon God's intention for man in the Holy Spirit. Nevertheless, it is questionable whether the necessary aspects of theology can be included under a term as specific as the Holy Spirit. Revelation and the life of the church are not possible apart from the Holy Spirit, but they are broader in meaning than the term "Holy Spirit" connotes. Because of the limitations of "ego-involvement under the Holy Spirit," a further theory awaits definition.

If certain descriptive terms could be selected and defined to symbolize the essential dimensions of the proposed theory, the basic step would be taken toward resolution of the problem. Here " symbol " means a word or words which in some sense participate in that to which they point. They would not be merely illustrative. They would bear a relationship to the truth that they communicate. The terms would become the focal point through which the data would be compressed and at the same time broadened to answer the concerns to be learned in Christian nurture.

It is proposed that this need is actualized in the term, *creation-engagement.* " Creative " would be more euphonious, but its use with " engagement " could mean just a more intensified, more imaginative, and more original form of human action. " Creation " is intended to communicate the divine participation while " engagement " symbolizes the active thrust of the whole person in learning. Justification is now offered for the selection of these terms in combination.

As translated from the Biblical Hebrew and Greek, " to create," or " creation " has theological significance. In the Old Testament, *barā'* means to shape, fashion, create, *but this is always a divine and never a human activity.*[2] God creates the heaven and the earth; mankind and man. (Gen., ch. 1; Isa. 45:12; Mal. 2:10.) New conditions and circumstances are also created. (Isa. 45:8; 57:18; Jer. 31:22.) Transformation whether of the person or the nonpersonal is the result of the creative work of God. He creates a clean heart in man (Ps. 51:10) and a new heaven and a new earth in the place of the old. (Isa. 65:17.)

In the New Testament, *poieō* is sometimes translated " create " in the sense of God's act, but it usually indicates man's doing or making. However, *ktizō* is always a sign of God's rather than man's work. The universe is created by God. (Rom. 1:25.) The Christian man is a new creation, a new man created in the likeness of God. (II Cor. 5:17; Gal. 6:15; Eph. 4:24.) Man is also created in Christ Jesus for good work. (Eph. 2:10.)[3]

Because "creation" is a word for God's act, to use it in a learning theory of Christian nurture is to free it as a symbol for the unique and essential power of God. Unlike the words "Holy Spirit," creation is not limited to the general power of God. "Creation" encompasses the full scope of God's participation in the concerns of Christian nurture. Instead of being drawn in at certain critical points, his creativity is presupposed as integral to the entire learning process.

As a word, "engagement" has particular meanings in various contexts.[4] For the machinist, engagement is the meshing of two or more gears. The gear teeth are interacting and interlocking with one another. There is the initial contact of the moving gear with the one which is stationary. When both gears are in motion, there is more of a mutual relationship. The second gear is in direct contact with the first, acting upon it even though the first gear is supplying the power. Engagement in military science is the encounter of two hostile forces in combat. There is a mutual address and response with weapons appropriate to the occasion. Combatants are expected to remain responsible to the task assigned. In the business and the professional world, engagement is the keeping of mutually designated appointments and services. The decision to be present at a particular time and place is a responsible commitment to be held in honor. Sociologically, engagement is a pledge of faithfulness between a man and a woman looking forward to the wider responsibility of marriage. Rightly appreciated, it is the "I" addressing the "Thou" in the free acceptance of obligations that the new relationship implies. Now because engagement includes such meanings as interaction, encounter, commitment, and mutually accepted responsibilities, it is able to integrate the essential insights of learning theory.

With this rationale for creation-engagement, the way is opened for a basic definition of the learning process in

Christian nurture. *The concerns of Christian nurture are learned as God creates new selves through the engagement of persons with their field of relationships.*

Creation-engagement means that the human learner and God are in active relationship at every point in the learning process. Persons may and do learn attitudes, values, and skills without reference to God. But the particular attitudes, values, and skills of the Christian faith are not learned except as God is a co-participant. Creation-engagement seeks to reclaim learning as a relational experience in which the learner is active rather than passive, intelligent rather than stupid, and reasonably free rather than determined.

## Creation-Engagement and the Common Concerns

In order to provide a vehicle for exposition and concurrently for comparison with the other theories, the same common concern categories will be utilized. Creation-engagement interpretations are given for responses in learning, the learner in learning, the context of learning, and the dynamics of learning.

*Responses are actions appropriate to the learner's engagement of the field of relationships under the creative impulse of God.* While the recurrence of responses similar in character to those which resulted from the initial engagement is affirmed, learning as a rigid causality following from certain stimuli is denied.

Unlike the stimulus-response interpretations of responses as necessary consequences of connections with stimuli, creation-engagement predicts similar responses in terms of probability. This cannot be otherwise since there is a free self grappling with responses to the particular field. In agreement with cognitive theory, creation-engagement considers responses as resulting from a restructuring of the field of relationships. Unlike cognitive theory, the Holy Spirit in revelation and the church is acknowledged as essential for the learning of responses in the Christian faith.

Creation-engagement views responses to be more than recurring actions in relationship with the tangible world of events, situations, things, and persons. The most basic learning is a response to revelation. This is more than a knowledge gained as a human achievement. God grasps the learner and gives him the insight to perceive wider implications of the revelation received. Responses to revelation are personal rather than universal. While the individual is aware of being a member of the covenant community, the responses to revelation are uniquely his own and to be expressed with due regard to his needs, the time and place of his life.

Responses are also to relationships. They are evidences of learning. In creation-engagement, responses may be muscular movements as the learner develops a style of life appropriate to his meeting with God. If the field of relationships at the moment is primarily intellectual, the responses may be cognitions related to man in the Biblical drama. The responses may be at the level of volition where a decision is made cutting across ordinary desires. Commitment to Jesus Christ expressed in a specific task is a response of this type. At other times, the response may be profoundly emotional. This is likely to be the case where the learner perceives the implications of sin and grace existentially. Here God has addressed the self and has elicited the responses of repentance and gratitude.

In general learning theory, the learned responses are functions of the intellectual capacity of the learner, his needs, and certain intervening variables. They are relevant in creation-engagement as well. Beyond these modifying factors for possible responses, there is the attempt to acknowledge the distorting power of sin. Even though its effects cannot be measured, it is enough to know that because the world of persons and things is under the judgment of sin, a consideration of learned responses as human works is inadequate. The human and situational factors may be at the optimum. Yet the planned responses of love and obedience may not occur. The educator is disappointed and is likely to remain in this state as long as his theory of learning presupposes control over responses. If as in creation-engagement, man as sinner is found in relationship with God as redeemer, the theory is brought into line with the evidences at hand. Where there is the learner as sinner, there is also the re-creative power of God issuing in a new self.

*The learner is an active, intelligent, responsible but sinful self to be understood through observation, self-perceptions, the quality of his relationships and revelation.* It is apparent that creation-engagement is broad in its admitted sources for gaining knowledge of the learner. Pathways to truth need not be circumscribed. In contrast, behaviorism is less objective than it purports to be. Truth of man as learner is accepted only if it has been acquired through careful observation of controlled conditions. For creation-engagement, all knowledge of man learned through scientific studies is gratefully accepted. But observation is just one of possible sources of knowledge. Because man is a person, it is permissible and legitimate to utilize man's reflections about himself as indicators of his perceptions, aspirations, feelings, and needs. The learner has an interior life of his own that is worthy of consideration.

Another source of knowing the learner is the depth and breadth of his relationships. The infant is probably not a self at birth. The young child becomes a self as he encounters the limiting effects of the world, of other persons, and of God. Neither is the attainment of selfhood a fixed or final point in a series of steps. The self is in a continual state of becoming according to how its relationships are engaged. This does not mean, however, inevitable progress. The quality of relationships may result in a stunting of the self. But as a theory of Christian learning, becoming is understood as the dynamic growth of the person in relationship with God. In the process, man receives impressions, "feedback," from his relationships. Apart from man's response to the perceived meanings of these relationships, man does not learn. His perceptions are in constant correction, of course, through the dialogic relation of revelation.

To describe the learner as a self is to acknowledge him as a being with both creaturely and divinely oriented needs yet without any implication of priority. Learning exists as a possibility from the human perspective to the degree that the learner is willing to take steps to maintain and enhance his nature. This is described as "readiness" in learning-theory literature. It is a valid observation if its dimensions are widened. Persons learn the ramifications of the Christian faith at the point where they are physically, psychologically, intellectually, and spiritually ready to engage and to be engaged in their field of relationships. Usually, readiness is not a static condition. Because it is often as personal as the learner himself, readiness fluctuates. In a classroom, the teacher cannot assume each person is physically ready for learning. There may be innumerable physical factors that prevent the learner from being engaged. Some of these are a lack of sleep, the experiences of pain, discomfort, hunger, and, if the learner is young, a need for movement. Psychological readiness is similar in nature. Persons may be physically but not psychologically ready for learning experiences. Perceptions of the self as incapable of learning, or anxiety about the person's role in the classroom, may prevent learning at the moment. If the perceptions become altered in a positive direction, the learner may become psychologically ready. Intellectual readiness is likely to be a more stable state. The given capacity does not change but intellectual readiness is dependent upon a grasp of prior learnings. Now there is nothing to hinder engaging in more advanced learning tasks. The kindergarten child understands the threat of judgment and the grace of redemption but is incapable of pursuing the theological concepts themselves. Spiritual readiness is dependent upon both the cultural values held by persons in the learner's field of relationships and upon the decision of God. In the freedom of the divine initiative in revelation, the learner may become ready to learn the responses of faith, love, obedience, and commitment.

There is a restlessness about the human learner which is a consequence of his divine orientation. He is not satisfied with the world of objects. The learner wishes to find and to participate in values that endure. He desires to be in relationship above himself and beyond the world of persons. Not only does the learner struggle to overcome barriers that prevent him from being at one with God but also those which are threats to his mastery of existence. Creation-engagement portrays the learner as intelligent and purposeful. His learned actions hold promise of goal realization. These are hypotheses to be tested.

If the learner is divinely related and actively intelligent, he is also responsible. Whether he learns the concerns of the Christian faith is no small matter. It is an issue related to God's intention for man as his covenant partner. There is the potential of judgment in terms of both a willingness to become engaged in the field of relationships and in the way the experiences are organized. The learner cannot take refuge in a naturalistic determinism. He stands before God as a responsible being and therefore, automatic behavior is maintained in its proper place. It is a factor in human learning but not the dominant one.

Because creation-engagement tries to be serious about the full evidence related to the description of the learner, it affirms that he is a sinner. Implied in this affirmation is a qualification about the effectiveness of learning tasks pursued independently of God. The learner's sin must modify the depth of learning. Without God's creative work, human learning is never able to go beyond the reaches of man's mind. Only God can overcome the sin of the learner. With God, the learner's classifications and perceptions may issue in responses more in accordance with the Christian revelation.

*The context of learning is the church* (the covenant community, the body of Christ, the fellowship of the Holy Spirit) *through which the learner engages his personal and nonpersonal field of relationships.* This description involves four interrelated elements which may be schematized as four concentric circles. Beginning at the center circle and moving outward, these elements are: the learner, the learner's relationships, the church, and God.

The learner exists as the center of experience. He is his context. Unless he organizes his relationships according to his interests and needs, there can be no learning. What the learner perceives is what is learned. The learning may be what is objectively desired or it may be the opposite. But learning is always something that happens in an individual through his conscious and unconscious perceptions. In creation-engagement, the contextual emphasis is upon the conscious involvement of the learner. It is not presumed that nurture occurs without effort. The learner acts, for example, upon the Biblical witness, the life of the church, and the treasury of devotional literature. Materials or experiences inconsistent with perceptions of the self are rejected and consequently remain unlearned. Experiences admitted to awareness are organized in relationship to the self. Now the way is opened to that radical learning peculiar to the creative action of God.

Although the learner is the center of experience, he cannot be the center unless there is an outside. He exists in the midst of relations. These are both personal and nonpersonal. The latter are such relations as the natural world, events, facts, signs, and symbols. As these are utilized by the self, skills are acquired, interpretations are developed, knowledge is organized, and reality is perceived. The nonpersonal relations establish limits for the self. As these are overcome and modified, they become part of the self-structure. This fact is expressed through the creation account in Gen., ch. 2. Man is placed in the midst of the Garden of Eden. To him are brought all the living creatures. He acquires an understanding of himself as he specifies their identities through the giving of names. Furthermore, the tree of temptation confronts man with another relation to be accepted or rejected. Through the decision demanded, selfhood is in process.

Personal relations as the wider context of learning are even more significant for changes in the self. Creation-engagement recognizes that the type of interpersonal relations outside the church modifies the kind of learning possible inside the church. Social and cultural values embodied in persons within the learner's environment are largely determinative of the perceptions that will be admitted to awareness. Because of interpersonal relations, meanings may be distorted and falsely symbolized. This is the case where the only father figure in the learner's experience is a man who is always denying legitimate aspirations and administering corporal punishment without regard for redemption. " Father " is now symbolized as a negative word whether for God or for men. Conversely, in other situations " father " may be correctly symbolized to include the steadfast love expected of God the Father Almighty. In creation-engagement, interpersonal relations are held to be the essential matrix in which God's self-disclosure may be heard and believed.

The third concentric circle is the church. Certainly, the church is made up of persons, or it is nothing. However, here the emphasis is more upon the nature of the church than upon its expression in persons. The church is the body of Christ, the redemptive community. It may be the Christian home if the life there is considered as part of the people of God. Facts may be learned in other contexts than the church, but if learning is separated from the worshiping congregation, there is less likelihood of change in the self through encounter with God. This does not mean that he is imprisoned in his church. He is free to effect changes in persons at any time and place, but God's people must not specify other places than the church because he has promised to be there in power.

God the Holy Spirit is the ultimate context for Christian nurture. Man realizes selfhood in relation with nonpersons and with persons, but the selfhood implied in man as a covenant partner of God is possible only in relationship with God. Here man realizes his destiny is to be recreated by Jesus Christ for a life of grateful obedience to God in the current life and the life beyond death.

*The dynamics of learning are operative as the learner is existentially motivated to engage and to restructure his field of relationships, and as these perceptual processes are utilized by the Holy Spirit to bring about encounter and response to Jesus Christ.*

It is possible to describe motivation in terms of needs common to mankind. Someone put it facetiously: "Every man needs food, shelter, and something to brag about!" Surely, there is need for physical and psychological security wherever people live. Persons are motivated to learn in order to achieve well-being. Actions that lead to satisfying expressions of security tend to be repeated. Those which do not yield maximum satisfaction are discontinued. Reinforcement theory builds on this valid observation. Reduction of tension is an appropriate description of motivation for man as a creature.

But such motivation is too general to be helpful for learning in Christian nurture. Descriptions of general needs reduce the learner to the status of object whereas the doctrine of man requires persons to be treated as subjects. Existential motivation includes the tendency for drive reduction, but motivation is considered more related to the self than reinforcement theory is prepared to affirm. The crucial motivation is involvement or enrichment of the self. There is an inner life of the self that determines the direction of action. If the action is admitted as being potentially useful to the self-structure, tension systems are set in operation to fulfill the demands of the personal condition. The self is sovereign, and humanly speaking, functionally autonomous. This is the critical dividing line between existential and deficit motivation. The former begins with the person rather than with observations about him. It arises at the point where through the Holy Spirit the self perceives that the Christian faith touches on issues of ultimate significance. Here motivation reaches crisis proportions. These conditions of crisis may arise at birth, adolescence, marriage, choice of vocation, death, sickness, and other challenges. They may come in the midst of a sudden awareness of sin or at a time of general disintegration of cultural values. It is the desperation of persons who have exhausted all their strength and at the moment are motivated to rely on the resources of God even though they are not yet certain who he is!

Once motivated, the learner becomes deeply rather than mechanically engaged in his field of relationships. Instead of concentrating upon parts, he begins with wholes. The broad relationships are perceived first and the specifics are dealt with later. It is the task of the instructor to provide learning tasks that help the learner to discover essential relationships without becoming bogged down in the minutiae. This is not the same as control of the learning situation as in conditioning. In the latter, the stimuli are provided to result in responses predetermined by the instructor. In creation-engagement, the instructor is the one to assist the learner in a learning task essentially personal. Once relationships have been perceived, meaning or insight may result. The mechanics of insight are not known, but it often occurs suddenly and dramatically.

From the human point of view, whether there is insight is dependent upon prior learning in Christian nurture. However, insight in itself is not wholly sufficient. Insight is not the dynamic for action. Persons may be able to comprehend essential relationships without the inclination to act. Something more is needed than insight. In the Holy

Spirit, God is at work modifying all the action processes of the learner. Insight is now no longer a human achievement. God is bringing about an encounter with himself in which he discloses who he is for the person's existential situation. In the transformation of insight, the self is changed. More risks are admitted to the self as necessary. Lives are gained in their loss for the gospel, and discipleship of Christ is claimed as man's chief end.

### Creation-Engagement and the Concerns to Be Learned

With the presentation of an over-all view of creation-engagement completed, there is the remaining task of seeing the theory in terms of its answers to the concerns to be learned in Christian nurture.

*Knowledge* of the mighty acts of God in Israel's history is learned as the learner is purposefully engaged by God in discovery and exploration of the basic documents of the church and as these are related to the learner's existential needs.

The learner is responding to the various relationships discerned in the Biblical drama. Necessary elements become learned as building blocks for intelligent discussion. Beyond the acquiring of facts, however, Israel's experience with God is perceived as significant for the learner's history. As he stands within the committed community, he is rehearsing events of the past, but these have immediate implications for his own pilgrimage of faith. A deeper kind of learning is occurring similar in nature to that suggested in the differentiation of terms for " knowledge " in some foreign languages. The French *savoir* and the German *wissen* refer to scientific knowledge. This is the kind of knowledge which general theories of learning are prepared to describe. The French *connaître* and German *kennen* indicate acquaintanceship and intimate personal participation in the common life.[5] Creation-engagement accounts for this latter kind of learning as well as the former.

Persons learn to *understand* the Bible as the drama of redemption as they receive divine-human guidance in the discernment of the essential relationships involved.

The Bible may be an incomprehensible book if it is pursued as a general reading adventure with a beginning and an end. The basic message may be obscured by the wealth of narratives and exhortations encountered. To maximize the development of understanding, persons must achieve facility in relating parts and wholes. At the same time, key ideas and events of the Bible need to become matters of concern to the learner. In creation-engagement, the learner reorganizes the Biblical ideas and events into new constellations of understanding. Specifically, he comes to discover that the theme of redemption is the one great idea which gives direction to the whole Biblical narrative.

The understanding possible for one existentially motivated within a committed community goes beyond structural rearrangement. Because God is involved, the achievement of understanding is his gracious gift.

The *attitude* of *agapē* love is learned as a response to revelation through the learner's engagement with the Biblical witness in the church and as that response is challenged in interpersonal relations.

To speak of *agapē* as a response to revelation indicates that love is learned indirectly. It is more than a subject for study. In the deep involvement with the Biblical witness, the learner is placed in a position where God's disclosure may be heard and believed. When the learner has heard of the greatness of God's steadfast love for the unlovely, *agapē* is likely to follow as the response most appropriate to revelation. If such incomprehensible love is learned as a response to revelation, it is also an experience within the church. Where persons can be accepted for what they are without threat of condemnation, they are in the position of privilege to learn *agapē*.

Nevertheless, love is only partially learned until it is

challenged through interpersonal relations that are out of sympathy with it. If the challenge is perceived as a locus of God's revelation in which he again addresses the learner and re-creates the response of love, there can be certitude about the learning of *agapē*. On the one hand, the learner comes to express love as his act but at the same time it is the result of God's transformation of his most prized self.

The church as *value* is learned as the learner recognizes himself to be in a state of estrangement from God and as the church is claimed as given by God for a witness to redemption and a community for nurture.

A common element in the answers of the four theories to the question of value learning is the need state of the learner. If the church meets the requirements of the learner, it is learned as value. Creation-engagement accepts the need state of the learner but defines the need in a transcendent context. Man is separated from God and cannot become related to him apart from his initiative. The intention of God is now expressed in the church. It is his gift and has intrinsic value.

However, the church is not perceived for what it is until the learner accepts the new relationship that awaits him in it. The acceptance is more than acquiescence. It is the conscious effort of the learner to participate in the redeeming and nurturing work of the church. The learner as self now perceives the church as essential to his self-structure. He must share his faith because he has beheld the glory of God within the community of redemption. God has been present transforming his conception of the church from a congenial organization engaged in acts of devotion to a divine society committed to the witness that God was in Christ reconciling the world to himself.

The *skill* of worship is learned as God confronts the learner through his engagement with the resources for Christian worship and his participation in the church as a worshiping fellowship.

The mechanical skills of worship can be learned according to any of the theories studied. Worship involves muscular movements. There is improvement with practice if attention is given to the cause of the errors and successes.

Yet the secular theories of learning are unable to define the fundamental element in worship as a skill. The learner's depth of motivation is not taken into consideration. The learner who has experienced God's redemption is under an inner compulsion to express his gratitude to God. This is not the same as a vague feeling of awe before an unknown deity. It is the conscious act of a responsible self acknowledging his relationship with God. An investigation of the resources for worship is now appropriate. Insight is gained into the meaning of devotion. With the insight received, the learner enters into a deeper sharing with the community at worship. Here God has chosen to meet the learner for the renewal of his life. Through God's disclosure of himself in the relationship, the skill-habit of worship is learned.

The *motive* of discipleship is learned through God's creative transformation of the learner's engagement with the church in the world.

Much of motivation in learning is doubtlessly deficit-oriented. The person does something to fill up a gap or to satisfy a need. But discipleship as a motive requires that the deficit be treated as not determinative. Persons must learn to serve Jesus Christ in the church and the world without regard for personal satisfaction as the primary concern. According to creation-engagement, this kind of motivation is learned only as the learner relates himself to human needs beyond his own, and as God redeems the continuing relationship. From one side, man has learned discipleship as an engagement of the will and the assumption of responsibility without qualification. From the other side, discipleship as a motive is the act of God. Unless the two are held together, discipleship may become the determination of the self to do something independently without a sense of deliberate relatedness to the One who alone causes the doing to be ultimately essential.

*Change in the self* occurs through the learner's engagement with witnesses to revelation, and as God reorganizes the learner's perceptual processes.

The self may be radically transformed through some conversion experiences. This conception of the change in the self-structure is beyond the range of learning theory because the transformation apparently is not related to nurture.

Christian nurture anticipates and predicts that the self may be changed through engagements with relationships that testify to God's historical disclosure in Israel and Jesus Christ, such as are given in the documents of the church as well as the church itself. In the view of creation-engagement, change in the self is a summary concern to be learned. This means that prior learnings of knowledge, understandings, attitudes, values, skills, and motives are both the means and the results of change in the self. The change is finally not under the control of man, however. It occurs as the Holy Spirit uses the various learning tasks to remind the learner of their existential significance. Without in any way removing the responsibility of the self in learning, persons come to realize in fact what they potentially are, God's new creation in Jesus Christ. Now the learners perceive and participate in their field of relationships from the perspective of the Holy Spirit.

This study has been intended as an introduction to the problem of learning in Christian nurture. It has been a venture in bridging the fields of Christian education, learning theory, and theology. The position taken is offered for evaluation and discussion to the end that nurture in the church may receive renewed consideration. The problem of learning is too great to go either by default or by uncritical acceptance. As the divine community in a broken world, the church is under obligation to be very serious about comprehending the nature of its nurture.

# Notes

## Introduction

1. " The psychology of animal learning – not to mention that of child learning – has been and still is primarily a matter of agreeing or disagreeing with Thorndike, or trying in minor ways to improve upon him. Gestalt psychologists, conditioned-reflex psychologists, sign-gestalt psychologists – all of us here in America seem to have taken Thorndike, overtly or covertly, as our starting point." Ernest R. Hilgard, *Theories of Learning,* 2d ed. (Appleton-Century-Crofts, Inc., 1956), p. 15. Quoted from E. C. Tolman, " The Determiners of Behavior at a Choice Point," *The Psychological Review,* Vol. 45 (1938), p. 11.

2. Hilgard, *op. cit.*

3. W. K. Estes, S. Koch, K. MacCorquodale, P. E. Meehl, C. G. Mueller, Jr., W. N. Schoenfeld, and W. Verplanck, *Modern Learning Theory* (Appleton-Century-Crofts, Inc., 1954).

## Chapter I. The Development of Christian Educational Theory

1. Carl Rogers, *Client-centered Therapy* (Houghton Mifflin Company, 1951), p. 15.

2. *What, Then, Is Man?* (Concordia Publishing House, 1958), p. 127.

3. Reuel Howe, *Man's Need and God's Action* (The Seabury Press, Inc., 1953), p. 9.

4. *Ibid.*, p. 21.

5. *Ibid.*, p. 73.

6. *Ibid.*, p. 57.

7. *Ibid.*, p. 112.

8. *Ibid.*, pp. 68–69.

9. *Ibid.*, p. 114.

10. Charles H. Johnson, "Christianity Is Learned," in *The Minister and Christian Nurture,* ed. by Nathaniel F. Forsyth (Abingdon Press, 1957), p. 64.

11. *Ibid.*, p. 73.

12. *Ibid.*, p. 83.

13. Iris Cully, *The Dynamics of Christian Education* (The Westminster Press, 1958), p. 119.

14. *Ibid.*, p. 120.

15. *Ibid.*, p. 143.

16. *Ibid.*, p. 155.

17. Jesse H. Ziegler, "Psychology of Religion and Religious Education," in *Religious Education: A Comprehensive Survey,* ed. by Marvin J. Taylor (Abingdon Press, 1960), pp. 34–43.

18. *Ibid.*, p. 35.

19. *Ibid.*, p. 41.

20. Randolph Crump Miller, *Education for Christian Living* (Prentice-Hall, Inc., 1956), p. 42.

21. Cf. Neal Miller, and John C. Dollard, *Social Learning and Imitation* (Yale University Press, 1941).

22. Randolph Crump Miller, *op. cit.*, p. 45.

23. D. Campbell Wyckoff, *Theory and Design of Christian Education Curriculum* (The Westminster Press, 1961).

24. *Ibid.*, pp. 102–103.

25. *Ibid.*, pp. 104–105.

26. *Ibid.*, p. 106.

27. *Foundations of Christian Teaching in Methodist Churches.* A Statement of the Curriculum Committee of the General Board of Education, The Methodist Church, 1960, p. 35.

28. *Ibid.*, pp. 35–36.

29. Howard Grimes, *The Church Redemptive* (Abingdon Press, 1958), pp. 90–91.

30. *Ibid.*, p. 92.

31. *Ibid.*, p. 93.

32. Lewis Joseph Sherrill, *The Gift of Power* (The Macmillan Company, 1958).

33. *Ibid.*, p. 148.

34. *Ibid.*, p. 148.

35. *Ibid.*, p. 161.

36. *Ibid.*, p. 152.

37. *Ibid.*, p. 153.
38. *Ibid.*, p. 156.

Chapter II. Concerns to Be Learned

1. Norman R. F. Maier, "The Premature Crystallization of Learning Theory," in *Learning Theory, Personality Theory and Clinical Research,* The Kentucky Symposium (John Wiley & Sons, Inc., 1954), p. 55.
2. Arthur W. Melton, "Present Accomplishment and Future Trends in Problem-Solving and Learning Theory," *American Psychologist,* Vol. 11 (1956), p. 280.
3. Hilgard, *op. cit.*, p. 12.
4. *Ibid.*, p. 458. Hilgard's "aspects of learning" appear to be similar to what I intend to communicate by "concerns to be learned."
5. Albert Bailey, "Philosophies of Education and Religious Education," in Taylor, ed., *op. cit.*
6. Cully, *op. cit.*, p. 44.
7. Howe, *op. cit.*, p. 95.
8. Paul Vieth, *Objectives in Religious Education* (Harper & Brothers, 1930), p. 186.
9. Eugene Nida, *Message and Mission* (Harper & Brothers, 1960).
10. Sherrill, *op. cit.*, p. 98.
11. Randolph Crump Miller, *op. cit.*, p. 63.
12. Sherrill, *op. cit.*, p. 66.
13. *Ibid.*, p. 69.
14. Howe, *op. cit.*, pp. 150–151.
15. Randolph Crump Miller, *op. cit.*, p. 55.
16. Cully, *op. cit.*, p. 171.
17. J. H. Oldham, *Florence Allshorn* (Harper & Brothers, 1951), p. 29.
18. Howe, *op. cit.*, p. 87.
19. Vieth, *op. cit.*, p. 215.
20. Charles H. Johnson, *loc. cit.*, p. 71.
21. Howe, *op. cit.*, p. 24.
22. Ernest Ligon, *Dimensions of Character* (The Macmillan Company, 1956), p. xii.
23. J. Donald Butler, *Four Philosophies and Their Practice*

*in Education and Religion,* rev. ed. (Harper & Brothers, 1957), p. 207.

24. *Ibid.,* p. 334.
25. *Ibid.,* p. 469.
26. Cully, *op. cit.,* p. 137.
27. Sherrill, *op. cit.,* p. 123.
28. Cully, *op. cit.,* p. 105.
29. Dietrich Bonhoeffer, *Life Together,* tr. by John W. Doberstein (Harper & Brothers, 1954), p. 56.
30. Cf. Sara Little, *Learning Together in the Christian Fellowship* (John Knox Press, 1956), p. 80.
31. Oldham, *op. cit.,* p. 63.
32. Vieth, *op. cit.,* p. 233.
33. Cf. George Webber, *God's Colony in Man's World* (Abingdon Press, 1960). An attempt to interpret the meaning of the church today with illustrations drawn from the interdenominational East Harlem Protestant Parish. The first chapter is appropriately titled "The Need for New Wineskins."
34. Randolph Crump Miller, *op. cit.,* pp. 265–266.
35. Nels F. S. Ferré, *Christian Faith and Higher Education* (Harper & Brothers, 1954), p. 154.
36. I am indebted to Sherrill, *op. cit.,* for "change in the self."
37. Cf. Butler, *op. cit.,* pp. 538–541.
38. Albert C. Outler, *Psychotherapy and the Christian Message* (Harper & Brothers, 1954), p. 69.
39. "Figure" refers to the particular perceptual object to which the perceiver gives his attention. By a slight shift in viewing, the same object is seen as something quite different from what it was formerly. The original object is now said to have become "ground." When the object has receded into ground, it is no longer perceptually present. Figure-ground may also be described as the relating of parts and wholes.
40. Risieri Frondizi, *The Nature of the Self* (Yale University Press, 1953), p. 177.

Chapter III. Representative Theories of Learning

1. G. T. Buswell, "Educational Theory and the Psychology of Learning," *The Journal of Educational Psychology,*

Vol. 47 (1956), pp. 175–184.

2. Donald Snygg, "Learning, An Aspect of Personality Development," in *Learning Theory, Personality Theory and Clinical Research,* The Kentucky Symposium, p. 130.

3. W. K. Estes, "Learning," in *Encyclopedia of Educational Research,* ed. by Chester W. Harris, 3d ed. (The Macmillan Company, 1960), p. 752.

4. Buswell, *loc. cit.*, p. 177.

5. Estes, *loc. cit.*, p. 752.

6. Snygg, *loc. cit.*, p. 130.

7. Arthur W. Combs and Donald Snygg, *Individual Behavior, A Perceptual Approach to Behavior,* rev. ed. (Harper & Brothers, 1959), p. 308.

8. Abraham Maslow, "Deficiency Motivation and Growth Motivation," in *Nebraska Symposium on Motivation,* ed. by Marshal R. Jones (University of Nebraska Press, 1955), p. 1.

9. Edward L. Thorndike, *The Psychology of Learning* (The Bureau of Publications, Columbia University Press, 1913), pp. 1–2.

10. *Ibid.*, p. 4.

11. Clark Hull, *A Behavior System* (Yale University Press, 1952), pp. 53–54.

12. *Ibid.*, p. 197.

13. Neal Miller and John C. Dollard, *Social Learning and Imitation,* p. 24.

14. *Ibid.*, p. 2.

15. *Ibid.*, p. 25.

16. *Ibid.*, p. 83.

17. E. R. Guthrie, *The Psychology of Learning,* rev. ed. (Harper & Brothers, 1952).

18. *Ibid.*, p. 289.

19. *Ibid.*, p. 44.

20. *Ibid.*, p. 62.

21. *Ibid.*, p. 47.

22. *Ibid.*, p. 91.

23. Wolfgang Köhler, *Gestalt Psychology* (Mentor Books, 1959; from the Liveright Copyright, 1947), p. 115.

24. Wolfgang Köhler, "Simple Structural Functions in the Chimpanzee and in the Chicken," in *A Source Book of Gestalt*

*Psychology,* ed. by Willis D. Ellis (Harcourt, Brace and Company, Inc., 1938), p. 226.

25. Charles E. Osgood, *Method and Theory in Experimental Psychology* (Oxford University Press, 1953), p. 608.

26. K. Koffka, *Principles of Gestalt Psychology* (Harcourt, Brace and Company, Inc., 1935), p. 110.

27. David Katz, *Gestalt Psychology,* tr. by Robert Tyson (The Ronald Press Company, 1950), p. 88.

28. Koffka, *op. cit.,* p. 440.

29. Jerome Bruner, *The Process of Education* (Harvard University Press, 1960), p. 7.

30. Koffka, *op. cit.,* p. 521.

31. Köhler, *Gestalt Psychology,* p. 192.

32. Edward C. Tolman, *Purposive Behavior in Animals and Men* (Appleton-Century-Crofts, Inc., 1932), p. 147.

33. Edward C. Tolman, "There Is More than One Kind of Learning," *The Psychological Review,* Vol. 56 (1949), p. 151. Here he is not really modifying his sign-gestalt theory but is raising the question of what different things are actually learned. A similar position is taken in this book under the term, "concerns to be learned." Therefore, major reliance is still placed on his basic work, *Purposive Behavior in Animals and Men.*

34. Tolman, *Purposive Behavior in Animals and Men,* p. 141.

35. *Ibid.,* p. 148.

36. Miller and Dollard, *op. cit.,* pp. 32–33.

37. Theodore Brameld, *Cultural Foundations of Education* (Harper & Brothers, 1957), p. 161.

38. Clyde Kluckhohn, *Mirror for Man* (Fawcett World Library, A Premier Reprint, 1957), p. 168.

39. *Ibid.,* p. 169.

40. Cf. Howard Kendler, "Reflections and Confessions of a Reinforcement Theorist," *The Psychological Review,* Vol. 58 (1951), p. 368.

41. Hull, *A Behavior System,* p. 112.

42. *Ibid.,* p. 108.

43. Clark Hull, "Knowledge and Purpose as Habit Mechanisms," *The Psychological Review,* Vol. 37 (1930), pp. 511–525.

44. Hull, *A Behavior System,* p. 152.

45. *Ibid.*, p. 321.

46. Miller and Dollard, *op. cit.*, p. 27.

47. Harry F. Harlow, "Motivational Forces Underlying Learning," in *Learning Theory, Personality Theory and Clinical Research,* The Kentucky Symposium, p. 52.

48. Maslow, *loc. cit.*, p. 22.

49. *Ibid.*, p. 14.

50. *Ibid.*, p. 18.

51. *Ibid.*, p. 20.

52. Gordon Allport, "Effect: A Secondary Principle of Learning," *The Psychological Review,* Vol. 53 (1946), p. 343.

53. *Ibid.*, p. 344.

54. Guthrie, *op. cit.*, p. 123.

55. *Ibid.*, p. 233.

56. O. Hobart Mowrer, "The Law of Effect and Ego Psychology," *The Psychological Review,* Vol. 53 (1946), pp. 321–334.

57. O. Hobart Mowrer, *Learning Theory and Personality Dynamics* (The Ronald Press Company, 1950), p. 293.

58. O. Hobart Mowrer, "Ego Psychology, Cybernetics and Learning Theory," in *Learning Theory, Personality Theory and Clinical Research,* The Kentucky Symposium, p. 83.

59. *Ibid.*, p. 90. Since these pages were written, I have learned that Mowrer has published a two-volume work on learning, but this discovery was made too late to be included here.

60. Thorndike, *op. cit.*, p. 349.

61. Hilgard, *op. cit.*, p. 45.

62. Hull, *A Behavior System,* p. 4.

63. Norman Maier, "The Premature Crystallization of Learning Theory," *Learning Theory, Personality Theory and Clinical Research,* pp. 55–56.

64. Virginia W. Voeks, "Acquisition of S–R Connections: A Test of Hull's and Guthrie's Theories," *The Journal of Experimental Psychology,* Vol. 47 (1954), p. 147.

65. Guthrie, *op. cit.*, p. 62.

66. John A. McGeoch, *The Psychology of Human Learning,* 2d ed., revised by Arthur L. Irion (Longmans, Green & Co., Inc., 1952), p. 62.

67. Harry Stack Sullivan, *The Interpersonal Theory of Psychiatry* (W. W. Norton & Company, Inc., 1953), p. 214.

68. Hilgard, *op. cit.*, p. 78.

69. Buswell, *loc. cit.*, p. 177.

70. John C. Bennett, *Christianity and Communism Today* (Association Press, 1960), p. 66.

71. Melville J. Herskovits, *Man and His Works* (Alfred A. Knopf, Inc., 1952), p. 491.

72. Mowrer, "Ego Psychology, Cybernetics and Learning Theory," *loc. cit.*, p. 84.

73. Gordon Allport, "The Ego in Contemporary Psychology," *The Psychological Review*, Vol. 50 (1943), p. 469.

74. Guthrie, *op. cit.*, p. 40. (Italics mine.)

75. Gordon Allport, *Becoming* (Yale University Press, 1955), p. 100.

76. Carl Rogers, *Client-centered Therapy*, p. 4.

77. Gordon Allport, *Becoming*, p. 15.

78. Koffka, *op. cit.*, pp. 320, 327.

79. Combs and Snygg, *Individual Behavior*, p. 309.

80. Rogers, *op. cit.*, p. 506.

81. Snygg, "Learning, An Aspect of Personality Development," *Learning Theory, Personality Theory and Clinical Research*, p. 134.

82. *Ibid.*, p. 135.

83. Rogers, *op. cit.*, p. 484.

84. J. Edward Dirks, "Teaching and Learning," *The Christian Scholar*, Vol. 44 (1961), p. 105.

85. Kurt Lewin, *A Dynamic Theory of Personality*, tr. by D. F. Adams, and K. Zener (McGraw-Hill Book Co., Inc., 1935), pp. 195–196.

86. Some of these are Gordon Allport, Arthur Combs and Donald Snygg, Carl Rogers and Kurt Lewin.

87. Tolman, *Purposive Behavior in Animals and Men*, p. 365.

88. *Ibid.*, pp. 176–179.

89. Osgood, *op. cit.*, p. 391.

90. Allport, *Becoming*, p. 15.

Chapter IV. Theological Foundations for Learning

1. James D. Smart, *The Teaching Ministry of the Church* (The Westminster Press, 1954), p. 12.
2. *Supra*, pp. 12, 13.
3. Edwin Lewis, *A Philosophy of the Christian Revelation* (Harper & Brothers, 1940), pp. ix–x.
4. Albrecht Oepke, *"Kalupto,"* in *Theologisches Wörterbuch zum Neuen Testament*, ed. by Gerhard Kittel (Stuttgart, Kohlhammer, 1938).
5. *Ibid.*, p. 575.
6. John Baillie, *The Idea of Revelation in Recent Thought* (Columbia University Press, 1956), p. 19.
7. Emil Brunner, *Revelation and Reason*, tr. by Olive Wyon (The Westminster Press, 1946), p. 23.
8. Karl Barth, *The Doctrine of the Word of God*, tr. by G. T. Thomson (Charles Scribner's Sons, 1936), p. 168.
9. Joseph H. Thayer, *A Greek-English Lexicon of the New Testament* (American Book Company, 1889).
10. Neal Miller and John C. Dollard, *Social Learning and Imitation*, p. 2.
11. Charles H. Johnson, "Christianity Is Learned," *The Minister and Christian Nurture*, p. 82.
12. Barth, *op. cit.*, p. 217.
13. Baillie, *op. cit.*, p. 64.
14. Howe, *Man's Need and God's Action*, p. 72.
15. George S. Hendry, "Revelation," in *A Theological Word-Book of the Bible*, ed. by Alan Richardson (London, S.C.M. Press, Ltd., 1950), p. 197.
16. Kenneth Cragg, *The Call of the Minaret* (Oxford University Press, 1956), p. 278.
17. Paul Tillich, *Systematic Theology I* (University of Chicago Press, 1951), p. 127.
18. Martin Buber, *Between Man and Man*, tr. by Ronald Gregor Smith (The Beacon Press, Inc., 1955), p. 35.
19. Paul Tournier, *The Meaning of Persons*, tr. by Edwin Hudson (Harper & Brothers, 1957), p. 165.
20. Tillich, *op. cit.*, p. 125.
21. *Ibid.*, p. 130.
22. Charles R. Stinnette, *Faith, Freedom and Selfhood* (The

Seabury Press, Inc., 1959), p. 130.

23. J. Donald Butler, "The Christian View of Man and the Meaning of Freedom and Authority in Education," *Religious Education,* Vol. 48 (1953), pp. 397–401.

24. *Ibid.,* p. 397.

25. Emil Brunner, *Man in Revolt,* tr. by Olive Wyon (The Westminster Press, 1947), p. 102.

26. Cf. *ibid.,* p. 292.

27. Edmond Jacob, "Man," in *A Companion to the Bible,* ed. by J. J. von Allmen, p. 248.

28. Reinhold Niebuhr, *The Nature and Destiny of Man* (Charles Scribner's Sons, 1941), I, p. 15.

29. T. F. Torrance, *Calvin's Doctrine of Man* (London, Lutterworth Press, 1949), pp. 29–30.

30. Stinnette, *op. cit.,* p. 170.

31. Johnson, *loc. cit.,* p. 64.

32. H. Mehl-Koehnlein, "Man," in *A Companion to the Bible,* ed. J. J. von Allmen (Oxford University Press, 1958), p. 252.

33. Walter Eichrodt, *Man in the Old Testament,* tr. by K. and R. Gregor Smith (London, S.C.M. Press, Ltd., 1951), p. 13.

34. *Ibid.,* p. 21.

35. *Ibid.,* p. 27.

36. Tournier, *op. cit.,* p. 193.

37. Buber, *op. cit.,* p. 45.

38. Suzanne de Dietrich, *God's Unfolding Purpose,* tr. by Robert McAfee Brown (The Westminster Press, 1960), p. 39.

39. Reinhold Niebuhr, *op. cit.,* p. 263.

40. Howe, *op. cit.,* p. 24.

41. Eichrodt, *op. cit.,* p. 51.

42. Reinhold Niebuhr, *op. cit.,* II, p. 49.

43. Brunner, *Man in Revolt,* p. 329.

44. Sherrill, *op. cit.,* pp. 45–46.

45. Karl Ludwig Schmidt, "The Church," in *Bible Key Words,* ed. and tr. by J. R. Coates (Harper & Brothers, 1951), p. 24.

46. Lesslie Newbigin, *The Household of God* (Friendship Press, 1954), p. 21.

47. Ph. Menoud, "Church," in *A Companion to the Bible,*

ed. by J. J. von Allmen, p. 51.

48. F. W. Dillistone, *The Structure of the Divine Society* (The Westminster Press, 1951), pp. 33–34.

49. *Ibid.*, p. 78.

50. Newbigin, *op. cit.*, p. 48.

51. Tournier, *op. cit.*, p. 89.

52. Stinnette, *op. cit.*, p. 135.

53. Howard Grimes, *The Church Redemptive,* p. 89.

54. Basil A. Yeaxlee, "Religion in the Schools," *Religious Education,* Vol. 56 (1961), p. 123.

55. Newbigin, *op. cit.*, p. 64.

56. Dillistone, *op. cit.*, p. 106.

57. *Ibid.*, p. 15.

58. *Ibid.*, p. 30.

59. *Ibid.*, p. 58.

60. *Ibid.*, p. 66.

61. *Ibid.*, pp. 67–68.

62. Sherrill, *op. cit.*, pp. 80–81.

63. Ph. Menoud, "Holy Spirit," in *A Companion to the Bible,* ed. by J. J. von Allmen, p. 171.

64. Samuel Shoemaker, *With the Holy Spirit and With Fire* (Harper & Brothers, 1960), p. 47.

65. J. Robert Nelson, *The Realm of Redemption* (London, The Epworth Press, 1951), p. 43.

66. Norman Snaith, *The Distinctive Ideas of the Old Testament* (The Westminster Press, 1944), p. 182.

67. Nelson, *op. cit.*, p. 53.

68. Arnold Come, *Human Spirit and Holy Spirit* (The Westminster Press, 1959), p. 169.

69. Shoemaker, *op. cit.*, pp. 33–34.

70. Menoud, "Holy Spirit," in *A Companion to the Bible,* p. 171.

71. Iris Cully, *The Dynamics of Christian Education,* p. 144.

72. Bernard Ramm, *The Witness of the Spirit* (Wm. B. Eerdmans Publishing Company, 1959), p. 84.

73. Jerome Bruner, *The Process of Education* (Harvard University Press, 1960), p. 59.

74. Snaith, *op. cit.*, p. 143.

75. *Ibid.*, p. 146.

76. *Ibid.*, p. 149.

77. *Ibid.*, p. 151.

78. George S. Hendry, *The Holy Spirit in Christian Theology* (The Westminster Press, 1956), p. 42.

79. *Ibid.*, p. 107.

80. Snaith, *op. cit.*, p. 184.

81. Hendry, *The Holy Spirit in Christian Theology,* p. 16.

82. *Ibid.*, p. 23.

83. F. W. Dillistone, *The Holy Spirit in the Life of Today* (The Westminster Press, 1947), p. 99.

84. Snaith, *op. cit.*, p. 181.

85. *Ibid.*, p. 181.

86. Hendry, *op. cit.*, pp. 25–26.

87. Cf. Nelson, *op. cit.*, p. 52.

88. Combs and Snygg, *Individual Behavior,* p. 154.

89. Menoud, "Holy Spirit," in *A Companion to the Bible,* p. 169.

90. Henry P. Van Dusen, *Spirit, Son, and Father* (Charles Scribner's Sons, 1958), p. 126.

91. *Ibid.*, pp. 82–83.

92. Tournier, *op. cit.*, p. 221.

Chapter V. A Theological Validation of Learning Theory

1. Barth, *The Doctrine of the Word of God,* p. 14.

2. H. Richard Niebuhr, *Christ and Culture* (Harper & Brothers, 1951), p. 69.

3. H. Poincaré, *The Foundations of Science,* tr. by George B. Halsted (Science Press, Inc., 1946), p. 30.

4. W. J. Brogden, "Some Theoretical Considerations of Learning," *The Psychological Review,* Vol. 58 (1951), p. 225.

5. *Supra,* p. 12.

6. *Supra,* p. 144.

7. Iris Cully, *The Dynamics of Christian Education,* p. 174.

8. *Supra,* p. 58.

Chapter VI. An Outline of a Theory

1. In this rejection, I nevertheless acknowledge my indebtedness to gestalt theory for its influence on my thinking.

2. Francis Brown, S. R. Driver, and Charles Briggs, eds.,

*A Hebrew and English Lexicon of the Old Testament* (Oxford, Clarendon Press, 1907; reprinted with corrections, 1957).

3. William Arndt, and F. Wilbur Gingrich, *A Greek-English Lexicon of the New Testament and Other Early Christian Literature* (The University of Chicago Press, 1957).

4. *Webster's New International Dictionary of the English Language,* 2d ed., unabridged (G. & C. Merriam Co., 1959).

5. Allen O. Miller, *Invitation to Theology* (Christian Education Press, 1958), p. 157.

# Index

## Names and Subjects

## Biblical References